International Summit on the Teaching Profession

Learning from the Past, Looking to the Future

EXCELLENCE AND EQUITY FOR ALL

Andreas Schleicher

This work is published under the responsibility of the Secretary-General of the OECD. The opinions expressed and arguments employed herein do not necessarily reflect the official views of OECD member countries.

This document, as well as any data and map included herein, are without prejudice to the status of or sovereignty over any territory, to the delimitation of international frontiers and boundaries and to the name of any territory, city or area.

The statistical data for Israel are supplied by and under the responsibility of the relevant Israeli authorities. The use of such data by the OECD is without prejudice to the status of the Golan Heights, East Jerusalem and Israeli settlements in the West Bank under the terms of international law.

Note by Turkey
The information in this document with reference to "Cyprus" relates to the southern part of the Island. There is no single authority representing both Turkish and Greek Cypriot people on the Island. Turkey recognises the Turkish Republic of Northern Cyprus (TRNC). Until a lasting and equitable solution is found within the context of the United Nations, Turkey shall preserve its position concerning the "Cyprus issue".

Note by all the European Union Member States of the OECD and the European Union
The Republic of Cyprus is recognised by all members of the United Nations with the exception of Turkey. The information in this document relates to the area under the effective control of the Government of the Republic of Cyprus.

Please cite this publication as:
Schleicher, A. (2021), *Learning from the Past, Looking to the Future: Excellence and Equity for all*, International Summit on the Teaching Profession, OECD Publishing, Paris, *https://doi.org/10.1787/f43c1728-en*.

ISBN 978-92-64-85849-7 (pdf)

International Summit on the Teaching Profession
ISSN 2312-7082 (print)
ISSN 2312-7090 (online)

Photo credits: Cover - © Monkey Business Images / Shutterstock.com; © Gorodenkoff / Shutterstock.com; Text - © Gorodenkoff / Shutterstock; © Monkey Business Images / Shutterstock; © DGLimages / Shutterstock

Corrigenda to publications may be found on line at: *www.oecd.org/about/publishing/corrigenda.htm*.
© OECD 2021

This work is available under the Creative Commons Attribution-NonCommercial-ShareAlike 3.0 IGO (CC BY-NC-SA 3.0 IGO). For specific information regarding the scope and terms of the licence as well as possible commercial use of this work or the use of PISA data please consult Terms and Conditions on www.oecd.org.

FOREWORD

The International Summit on the Teaching Profession (ISTP) 2021 brings ministers and union leaders together to explore how governments, teacher organisations and schools can work together. Specifically, the ISTP seeks to address five overarching questions:

- How do governments and teacher organisations come together to determine the broader, multi-dimensional measures of success that incorporate the whole child? How can we achieve these desired successes?

- Building on child development and learning sciences research, what is needed to support each person's learning (including academic knowledge and skills) with mental and physical health and social emotional learning?

- The well-being of students, teachers and other critical educators are precursors to improving education. How does the teaching profession best support student well-being?

- How do we value and support the teaching profession and support the well-being of teachers? What support do teachers need, including collaboration with other educators (such as support personnel) and other professions, in enhancing student well-being and mental health?

- How can governments and teacher organisations collaborate on strategies that are relentlessly focused on equity to advance the future of education and to ensure excellent education for all?

This report, *Learning from the Past, Looking to the Future: Excellence and Equity for all*, provides data and analysis from the OECD as background for ministers and union leaders to address these questions.

The report was written by Andreas Schleicher, with contributions from Karine Tremblay, Pablo Fraser, Lucie Cerna, Miho Taguma, and Esther Carvalhaes. It is based on data, comparative analysis and reports from the OECD.

Andreas Schleicher

Director for Education and Skills and Special Advisor on Education Policy to the Secretary-General

TABLE OF CONTENTS

FOREWORD 3
INTRODUCTION 6
EXECUTIVE SUMMARY 8

CHAPTER 1 WORKING TOGETHER TO REDEFINE EDUCATIONAL SUCCESS 11
New ways to defining new educational goals 12
Collaborative strategies to implement new educational goals 20
References 27

CHAPTER 2 SUPPORTING THE WHOLE CHILD 29
Strengthening student resilience and agency 30
Student well-being – and what teachers and parents can do to foster it 31
Supporting teachers so they can support students 40
References 44

CHAPTER 3 REDEFINING EQUITY IN THE 21ST CENTURY 45
Inclusive teaching: design elements to promote more equitable and
inclusive education 46
Promoting equitable and inclusive teaching strategies in the virtual classroom 49
Enhancing school-level collaboration to promote more equitable and
inclusive education for all 50
Allocating high-quality teachers to disadvantaged schools to promote more equitable
and inclusive education for all 52
Promoting teacher diversity to support the learning and
well-being outcomes of diverse students 53
Working towards equity in the distribution of staff across schools 54
References 56

FIGURES

Figure 1	COVID-19 infection rates, school closures and the performance of education systems	7
Figure 2.1	Young people care about climate change but feel unable to make a difference	32
Figure 2.2	A framework for student well-being	33
Figure 2.3	Student life satisfaction and its relationship with school factors (OECD average)	34
Figure 2.4	Student sense of belonging	35
Figure 2.5	Academic learning and life satisfaction	36
Figure 2.6	Teacher support in «happy» and «unhappy» schools (2015)	37
Figure 2.7	Teachers' sources of stress	41
Figure 2.8	Relationship between teachers' experience of stress at work and task intensity	42
Figure 2.9	Intention to leave teaching within the next five years related to work-related stress and satisfaction with the terms of employment	43

INFOGRAPHICS

Infographic 1.1	Portugal's students' profile by the end of compulsory schooling	24
Infographic 1.2	Student profile Korea	24
Infographic 1.3	Student profile Scotland (United Kingdom)	25
Infographic 1.4	Hong Kong (China) learning goals	26
Infographic 1.5	The Council of Ministers of Education, Canada's (CMEC) pan-Canadian global competencies	27

TABLES

Table 1.1	Educational goals and criteria for success in ISTP jurisdictions	12
Table 3.1	Three main elements for inclusive teaching	47
Table 3.2	Three main elements for inclusive teaching	48
Table 3.3	Inclusive teaching through online platforms	50
Table 3.4	Strategies to guide teachers through inclusive school leadership and management	51
Table 3.5	Strategies to match high-quality teachers to disadvantaged schools	52
Table 3.6	The impacts of teacher-student congruence	53

INTRODUCTION

THE FUTURE WILL ALWAYS SURPRISE US

The pandemic has heightened the urgency to strengthen the resilience of both learners and education systems to external disruptions. Students who knew how to learn and enjoyed learning, and who had access to alternative learning opportunities and an ecosystem of cognitive, social and emotional support were often able to find their way despite closed school doors. Not so for many other students as the crisis has amplified the many inadequacies and inequities in education systems.

What is true for individual students holds for education systems as well: Covid-19 infection rates in the populations of OECD countries during 2020 were largely unrelated to the number of days schools were closed during the year. Some countries were able to keep their schools open even in a difficult pandemic context. In contrast, the performance of 15-year-olds on the OECD Programme for International Student Assessment (PISA) correlates strongly with the extent of school closures in countries: the number of days schools were fully closed in 2020 accounts for 54% of the variation (and 31% after accounting for country GDP) (Figure 1). One interpretation is that notwithstanding the political nature of decisions on school closures, high-performing education systems with strong frontline capacity and greater institutional and systemic resilience were often able to maintain operations even amid severe disruptions. The importance of resilience and adaptability in education will only grow over time as the future continue to surprise us.

Importantly, the implications of disruptions are never predetermined. It is the nature of our collective responses to these disruptions that determines their outcomes – the continuous interplay between the social and technological frontier and the cultural, institutional and economic contexts and agents that education systems mobilise in response.

The current approach to schooling was invented in the industrial age, when the prevailing norms were standardisation and compliance, and when it was both effective and efficient to educate students in batches and train teachers once for their entire working lives. The curricula that spelled out what students should learn were designed at the top of the pyramid, then translated into instructional material, teacher education and learning environments – often through multiple layers of government – until they reached and were implemented by individual teachers in the classroom. This approach, inherited from the industrial model of work, was designed for the "average" student but does not address the needs of all students. In the 21st century, equity needs to go beyond treating students equally and uniformly. An equitable education is one that is impactful because it adapts to students' differences.

The old industrial approach to schooling also slows change in a fast-moving world. Societies are now evolving much more quickly than the structural capacity of our current education systems to respond. The way to address this is to build on the expertise of teachers and school leaders and involve them in the design of policies and practices that educate students effectively by adapting to their particular needs.

Introduction

This is not accomplished just by letting a thousand flowers bloom; it requires carefully crafted enabling environments that can unleash teachers' and schools' ingenuity and build capacity for change. It also requires system leaders to tackle institutional structures that are built too often around the interests and habits of adults rather than learners – leaders who listen to students, educators and communities; and leaders who are sincere about social change, imaginative in policy making, and capable of using the trust they earn to deliver effective reforms.

The rapid educational progress visible in some countries shows that universal high-quality education is an attainable goal. It is within our means to deliver a future for millions of learners who currently do not have one. The task is not to make the impossible possible but to make the possible attainable

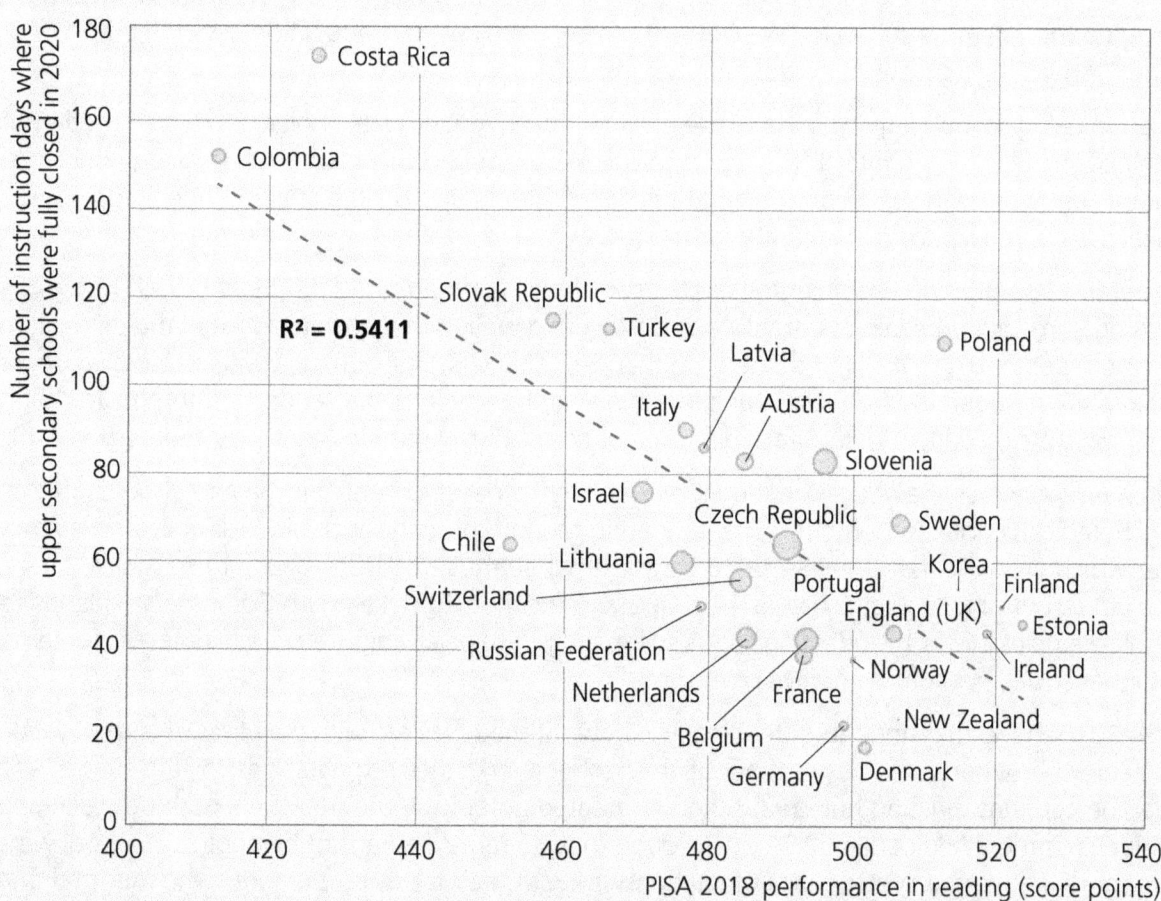

Figure 1 COVID-19 infection rates, school closures and the performance of education systems

Note: The size of the bubbles represents the number of COVID-19 cases per million inhabitants in 2020.
Source: (OECD, 2021[1]), *The State of School Education: One Year into the COVID Pandemic*, OECD Publishing, Paris, https://doi.org/10.1787/201dde84-en.

REFERENCES

OECD (2021), *The State of School Education: One Year into the COVID Pandemic*, OECD Publishing, Paris, https://doi.org/10.1787/201dde84-en. [1]

EXECUTIVE SUMMARY

If there are any preliminary lessons to be drawn from how the COVID-19 pandemic has impacted our school systems it is that education needs to pay closer attention to students' social and emotional well-being alongside cognitive development, and to equity in learning opportunities as well. Students with better all-round well-being and more advantageous socio-economic footing are likely to have navigated pandemic school closures better than others. How can education systems prepare for other disruptions that will come down the road?

Strengthening schools' equity and a whole-child approach requires stakeholders to work together to rethink curriculum. In Chapter 1, this report discusses how policy makers can help learners, educators, parents and communities recognise what needs to change and build a shared understanding and collective ownership for curriculum reform.

Chapter 1 lays out different countries and jurisdictions' learning goals. Some approach reform by revising curriculum/guidelines partially and on demand while others create space in the curriculum from the beginning to accommodate new changes rapidly. Digital curricula will enable even more rapid and less onerous changes. A guiding principle, however, is that education reform focus on core concepts that are valued in each discipline or across disciplines, and that they endure over time.

Chapter 2 explores the educational goal of whole-child development that balances the cognitive, psychological, social and physical. The pandemic has taught us how crucial resilience and agency are, which are skills that the PISA 2018 assessed: what are students' capacity to set goals, reflect and act responsibly to effect change? The OECD's Education 2030 Learning Compass has identified many examples in which student agency is successfully developed and exercised in different contexts, whether social, economic, creative or moral.

PISA 2018 shows that students differ greatly in how satisfied they are with their lives, their motivation to achieve, how anxious they feel about their schoolwork, their expectations for the future, and their perceptions of being bullied at school or treated unfairly by their teachers both between and within countries. Additionally, PISA 2015 found that students' feelings of belonging at school were strongly linked to their perceptions of relationships with their teachers. Students who reported that their teacher was willing to provide help and was interested in their learning were about 1.3 times more likely to feel that they belong at school. To help teachers better connect with their students, professional development could focus more on classroom and relationship management.

When students feel they fit in at school they are able to perform better academically and be more motivated. Bullying derails this. On average across OECD countries, around 11% of students reported that they are frequently (at least a few times per month) made fun of, 7% reported that they are frequently left out of things, and 8% reported that they are frequently the object of nasty rumours in school. Around 4% of students – roughly one per class - reported that they are hit or pushed at least a few times per month, a percentage that varies from 1% to 9.5% across countries.

Executive Summary

This is something schools can work on. They can move more effectively against bullying by fostering an environment of safety, tolerance and respect for children. This includes training for teachers on bullying behaviour and how to handle it, and strategies to provide information to and engage with parents.

School closures during the pandemic brought school leaders and teachers closer to families to coordinate students' learning. Schools can build on this relationship and enlist parents in the fight against bullying and students' well-being in general.

We see that school leaders, and teachers, especially, are central to students' feeling at ease at school but to be at their best, their own well-being needs to be understood. Teaching and Learning International Survey (TALIS) 2018 shows that 49% of teachers indicated "having too much administrative work to do" was the top source of stress. Some 69% of schools leaders reported the same. And teachers who spend many hours doing administrative tasks are more likely to report high levels of stress than those who spend many hours teaching in the classroom. Administrative burden needs to be addressed. Staff participation in school governance and support for continuous professional development is another top teacher concern: TALIS analyses show that they are strongly related to teachers' satisfaction with their terms of employment (apart from salary), and, ultimately, their willingness to stay in the job.

Chapter 3 focuses on how education systems can strengthen equity. The pandemic has thrown a spotlight on inequities at the individual, institutional and systemic levels, whether it is disadvantaged students with poorer access to information and communications technology (ICT) equipment, Internet and a quiet place to do their schoolwork or countries with the lowest educational performance tending to close their schools for longer periods of time in 2020.

Pandemic aside, education provides a unique lever to address the sources of inequality and foster social mobility. Education systems have been emphasising inclusive access but now the challenge is to ensure inclusive success. Fundamentally, inclusive school leadership and management can set collaborative school environments that adequately support inclusive teaching practices. Chapter 3 provides several country examples of school-level collaborative culture. Teacher diversity needs to be promoted. So does diversity in teaching and learning. The pandemic has shown that online learning can broaden and deepen education's reach but teachers' involvement in training to use online tools and even the development of remote platforms needs to continue.

Schools in disadvantaged settings need additional support. The design and implementation of equitable and transparent funding allocation mechanisms that balance targeted and regular funding is important. So is the need to make effective teachers available to schools that need them the most. There are diverse mechanisms that match high-performing teachers with schools in difficulty. Education systems can review regulations for the selection and transfer of teachers to create greater flexibility for appointments regardless of employment status or experience. Another policy worth exploring is various incentives that make disadvantaged schools more attractive to effective teachers. Financial incentives are one; recognising teachers' experience in difficult or remote schools for their career progression is another.

01
WORKING TOGETHER TO REDEFINE EDUCATIONAL SUCCESS

How do governments and teacher organisations come together to determine the broader, multi-dimensional measures of success that incorporate the whole child? And how can we achieve these desired successes?

NEW WAYS TO DEFINING NEW EDUCATIONAL GOALS

Over recent years, the educational goals, curricula and student profiles of countries and jurisdictions have increasingly embraced a "whole child" perspective, looking comprehensively at dimensions of knowledge, skills, attitudes and values jointly with the well-being of students (see the summary in Table 1.1 for jurisdictions participating in the ISTP 2021 with available data).

Discussions on learning goals and student profiles also take place at the international level, as illustrated in the co-creation of the OECD Learning Compass 2030. Over the last four years, governments, representatives from OECD's Trade Union Advisory Council, teachers, school leaders, teacher educators, students, non-governmental organisations, private enterprises and other stakeholders in civil society have come together to outline a future vision for education, reaffirming broader goals of education and children's and students' multi-dimensional successes in both learning and well-being.

Table 1.1 [1/8] Educational goals and criteria for success in ISTP jurisdictions

Country/ jurisdiction	Student profile
Australia	• Successful lifelong learners • Confident and creative individuals • Active and informed members of the community
British Columbia (Canada)	The Educated Citizen is: • thoughtful, able to learn and to think critically, and who can communicate information from a broad knowledge base • creative, flexible, self-motivated and who have a positive self-image • capable of making independent decisions • skilled and who can contribute to society generally, including the world of work • productive, who gain satisfaction through achievement and who strive for physical well-being • cooperative, principled and respectful of others regardless of differences • aware of the rights and prepared to exercise the responsibilities of an individual within the family, the community, Canada, and the world
Czech Republic	• to make it possible for pupils to acquire learning strategies and to motivate them to lifelong learning • to stimulate creative thinking, logical reasoning and problem solving in pupils • to guide pupils towards engaging in effective and open communication on all possible issues • to develop pupils' ability to cooperate and to respect their own as well as others' work and achievements • to prepare the pupils to manifest themselves as independent, free and responsible individuals who exercise their rights and meet their obligations • to create in pupils the need to express positive feelings in their behaviour and conduct when undergoing various situations in life; to develop in them perceptiveness and sensitive relations towards other people, the environment and nature • to teach pupils to develop their physical, mental and social health actively, protect it and be responsible for it • to guide pupils towards tolerance of and consideration for other people, their cultures and spiritual values, to teach them to live together with others • to help pupils to become familiar with and develop their own abilities according to their realistic possibilities and to utilise them along with their acquired knowledge and skills when making decisions on their own life and professional orientations

Source: (OECD, 2021[2]) *Future of Education and Skills 2030, Policy Questionnaire on Curriculum Redesign (PQC)* (2021), item 1.1.2. https://www.oecd.org/education/2030-project/curriculum-analysis/data/.

Table 1.1 [2/8] Educational goals and criteria for success in ISTP jurisdictions

Country/jurisdiction	Student profile
OECD Denmark	Knowledge and skills that will: • prepare them for further education and training and instil in them the desire to learn more • familiarise them with Danish culture and history • give them an understanding of other countries and cultures • contribute to their understanding of the interrelationship between humans and the environment and promote the well-rounded development of the individual pupil • enable students to develop awareness, imagination, self-efficacy, a background for forming opinions and taking action • prepare the students for participation, responsibility, understanding their rights and duties in a free and democratic society
Estonia	• understand the values underlying their actions • sense responsibility for the consequences of their actions • have an understanding of their future roles in family, working life, society and the state • knows the generally recognised values and moral principles in society, follows them in school and outside school, who does not remain indifferent when they are flouted, and intervenes in accordance with his or her abilities when necessary • knows and honours his or her language and culture, and contributes to the preservation and development of the Estonian language and culture; has a conception and knowledge of different cultures of the world, respects people from other ethnicities • is intellectually curious, knows how to study and find opportunities for further study, using relevant advice if necessary • is enterprising, believes in him or herself, shapes his or her ideals, sets goals for him or herself and acts in their name, makes adjustments to his or her behaviour and takes responsibility for his or her actions • has the ability to clearly and relevantly express him or herself, taking into account situations and partners in communication; to present and justify their positions; to understand and interpret different types of texts; knows and follows the rules of orthography • is proficient in at least one foreign language at a level that allows him or her to communicate in writing and orally, and to read and understand age-appropriate foreign-language texts • is capable of resolving issues arising in various fields in everyday life that require use of mathematical thinking methods (logical thinking and spatial reasoning) and presentation methods (formulae, models, diagrams, graphs) • understands the interrelations between humans and the environment, takes a responsible attitude to the environment and lives and acts in an environmentally sustainable manner • knows how to pose natural science questions, discuss them, present scientific positions and make conclusions on their basis • is able to get by in the world of technology and use technology for the designated purpose and with as little risk as possible • is an active and responsible citizen who is interested in the democratic development of one's school, home region and the state • is able to express him or herself creatively, has respect for art and cultural heritage • values and follows a healthful lifestyle and is physically active • thinks systematically, creatively and critically, is open to self-development

Source: (OECD, 2021[2]) *Future of Education and Skills 2030, Policy Questionnaire on Curriculum Redesign (PQC)* (2021), item 1.1.2. https://www.oecd.org/education/2030-project/curriculum-analysis/data/.

Table 1.1 [3/8] **Educational goals and criteria for success in ISTP jurisdictions**

Country/ jurisdiction	Student profile
Finland	Uniqueness of each pupil and right to a good education: • unique and valuable just as he or she is • full potential as a human being and a member of society • identity, their understanding of humanity, worldview and philosophy of life and place in the world • understand themselves, other people, the society, the environment and different cultures • lifelong learning, which is an elemental part of building a decent life • building their personal value systems, humanity, knowledge and ability, equality and democracy • human being who strives for truth, goodness, beauty, justice and peace • able to address conflicts between aspirations and the current reality ethically and sympathetically, and having the courage to stand up for what is good and part of knowledge and ability • capable of making decisions based on ethical reflection, putting themselves in the place of another person, and consideration based on knowledge • think about what is valuable in life: attitudes to ourselves, other people, the environment and information, in the ways we act and in our willingness to take action • strive to act correctly and show respect for themselves, other people and the environment • are able to use information critically • strive towards self-regulation and accepting responsibility for own development and well-being as also part of general knowledge and ability • defend values of respect for life and human rights and to appreciate the inviolability of human dignity • well-being, democracy and active agency in civil society • Cultural diversity as a richness: • personal cultural identity and active actors in their own culture and community while promoting their interest in other cultures • creativity and respect for cultural diversity and promotes interaction within and between cultures, thus laying a foundation for culturally sustainable development Necessity of a sustainable way of living: • eco-social knowledge and ability is creating ways of living and a culture that foster the inviolability of human dignity and the diversity and ability for renewal of ecosystems while building a competence base for a circular economy underpinned by sustainable use of natural resources • responsibility to steer technology in a direction that safeguards the future of humans and the environment • cross-generational global responsibility

Source: (OECD, 2021[2]) *Future of Education and Skills 2030, Policy Questionnaire on Curriculum Redesign (PQC)* (2021), item 1.1.2. https://www.oecd.org/education/2030-project/curriculum-analysis/data/.

Table 1.1 [4/8] Educational goals and criteria for success in ISTP jurisdictions

Country/ jurisdiction	Student profile
OECD Ireland	Skills and thinking abilities: • apply their learning in a number of different contexts • engage in research, investigation and experimentation • gather and synthesise information • think analytically and solve problems • be creative, entrepreneurial and innovative • work independently and/or as part of a team • make decisions, implement ideas and take action • communicate and critically respond to text and dialogue • present and perform in a variety of modes • collaborate with others in the completion of tasks • think critically and reflect on their learning • engage in dialogue with their teachers and peers • evaluate their own learning, either as individuals or in collaboration with their peers Principles and key skills of the Junior Cycle: • Students being able to meet the challenges of life beyond school, of further education, and of working life • Inclusive education - equality of opportunity, participation and outcomes for all • Students participating, generating engagement and enthusiasm, and connecting with life outside the school • Capacity for future learning
Japan	• Independent individuals in social/professional: being able to have a broader perspective that is based on culture and tradition in own country and region, to have high aspirations and motivation to realise ideal, toward learning autonomously, to decide the necessary information, to deepen knowledge by themselves, to develop the personal style and competencies, to create their own life • Through a dialogue and discussion being able to show their opinions, the reasons why they think, to understand others' thoughts, to broaden and deepen their own thoughts, to develop opinions as a group, to collaborate with various people with consideration for others, • In a rapidly changing society, to be able to envision a better life and society as exercise sensibility richly, to find and solve problems by trial and error, to create new values and to proceed to find and solve new problems • Knowledge: wide-ranging knowledge and culture, to seek the truth, cultivate a rich sensibility and sense of morality, while developing a healthy body • Skills: the abilities of individuals while respecting their value, cultivate their creativity, foster a spirit of autonomy and independence, foster an attitude to value labour while emphasising the connections with career and practical life • Values: justice, responsibility, equality between men and women, mutual respect and co-operation, actively contribute, in the public spirit, to the building and development of society • Attitudes: respect life, care for nature, contribution to the protection of the environment, respect our traditions and culture, love the country and region that nurtured them, together with respect for other countries, a desire to contribute to world peace and the development of the international community

Source: (OECD, 2021[2]) *Future of Education and Skills 2030, Policy Questionnaire on Curriculum Redesign (PQC)* (2021), item 1.1.2. https://www.oecd.org/education/2030-project/curriculum-analysis/data/.

Table 1.1 [5/8] **Educational goals and criteria for success in ISTP jurisdictions**

Country/ jurisdiction	Student profile
OECD Korea	• self-directed person who builds a self-identity, explores a career and life, on the basis of holistic growth • creative person who discovers something novel by means of diverse ideas, challenges based upon basic abilities • cultivated person who appreciates and promotes the culture of humankind, on the basis of cultural literacy, understanding of diverse values • person who leads a life worthy of human dignity, abilities for independent life, lives in harmony with others, fulfilling the ethics of caring and sharing, support the realisation of an ideal of shared human prosperity, necessary qualities as democratic citizen contribute to the development of a democratic state with a sense of community and connection to the world under the humanitarian idea
Netherlands	• to become, independent, active and responsible citizens in a pluri-form and democratic society • to take a stand regarding social and political issues • to evaluate social and political issues • to value and respect differences between people
New Zealand	The Vision of The New Zealand Curriculum is for young people [who will be]: • Confident • Connected • Actively involved • Lifelong learners The Centrepost of Te Marautanga o Aotearoa is: • successful learners • who will grow as competent and confident learners • effective communicators in the Maori world • healthy of mind, body and soul • secure in their identity • sense of belonging

Northern Ireland (United Kingdom)	• Attitudes and Dispositions: Personal responsibility, concern for others, commitment, determination and resourcefulness, curiosity and openness to new ideas, self-belief, optimism and pragmatism, community spirit flexibility, tolerance, integrity, courage and respect
	• Values-related in respect of learning to make informed and responsible choices and decisions:
	  – as an individual in relation to personal understanding, mutual understanding, personal health, moral character and spiritual awareness)
	  – as a contributor to society in relation to citizenship, cultural understanding, media awareness and ethical awareness)
	  – as a contributor to the economy and environment (in relation in relation to the following key elements*- employability; economic awareness, sustainable development and environmental responsibility)
	• Learning for Life and Work/ Local and Global Citizenship is set out as an critical enquiry-based exploration of the values of: Diversity and Inclusion, Human Rights and Social Responsibility, Equality and Social Justice, Democracy and Active Participation
	• General curriculum framework expectations for young people: To achieve their potential, to make 'informed and responsible choices and decisions throughout their lives as individuals, contributors to society and contributors to the economy and environment'

Source: (OECD, 2021[2]) *Future of Education and Skills 2030, Policy Questionnaire on Curriculum Redesign (PQC)* (2021), item 1.1.2. https://www.oecd.org/education/2030-project/curriculum-analysis/data/.

Table 1.1 [6/8] **Educational goals and criteria for success in ISTP jurisdictions**

Country/ jurisdiction	Student profile
Norway	• Values: Human dignity, Identity and cultural diversity, Critical thinking and ethical consciousness, Creativity, engagement and urge to explore, Respect for nature and environmental awareness, Democracy and agency • Competencies: social learning and development, development of literacy skills (reading, writing, oral, numeral and digital skills), lifelong learning strategies. • Cross- disciplinary themes: Democracy and Citizenship, Sustainable Development, Public Health and Life Skill
Ontario (Canada)	• can achieve at high levels, acquire valuable skills and become engaged members of their communities • are fully engaged in their learning, building the skills and developing the attributes they will need to compete for and create the jobs of tomorrow. • benefit from a wide array of opportunities inside outside of school • regardless of the challenges they face, prepared to adapt, achieve, and excel • success in literacy, mathematics, science, the arts • higher-order skills: critical thinking, communication, collaboration, entrepreneurship
Poland	• efficient communication in Polish and in modern foreign languages • efficient use of mathematics tools in everyday life as well education of mathematical thinking • searching, ordering, critical analysis and use of information from various sources • creative problem solving in various areas with consciousness using methods and tools derived from information technology, including programming • solving problems, also using mediation techniques • team work and social activity • active participation in the cultural life of the school, the local environment and the country
Portugal	• equipped with multiple literacies that allow him/ her to analyse and question critically the reality, evaluate and select the information, formulate hypotheses and make informed decisions on a daily basis • free, autonomous, responsible and aware of him/ herself and the world that he/ she is surrounded by • able to deal with change and uncertainty in a rapidly changing world • recognises the importance and challenge offered in the Arts, Humanities and Science and Technology for the social, cultural, economic and environmental sustainability of Portugal and the world • able to think critically and autonomously, creatively, with competence to work collaboratively and communication skills • able to continue lifelong learning, as a decisive factor in the their personal development and their social intervention • knows and respects the fundamental principles of a democratic society and the rights, guarantees and freedoms on which it is based • values respect for human dignity, the exercise of citizenship in full solidarity with others, cultural diversity and for the democratic debate • to reject all forms of discrimination and social exclusion
Québec (Canada)	• educated and cultivated individuals • involved citizens • competent workers

Source: (OECD, 2021[2]) *Future of Education and Skills 2030, Policy Questionnaire on Curriculum Redesign (PQC)* (2021), item 1.1.2. https://www.oecd.org/education/2030-project/curriculum-analysis/data/.

Table 1.1 [7/8] Educational goals and criteria for success in ISTP jurisdictions

Country/ jurisdiction	Student profile
OECD Scotland (United Kingdom)	• Successful learners with enthusiasm and motivation for learning, determination to reach high standards of achievement, openness to new thinking and ideas and able to use literacy, communication and numeracy skills, use technology for learning, think creatively and independently, learn independently and as part of a group, make reasoned evaluations, link and apply different kinds of learning in new situations • Confident individuals with self-respect, a sense of physical, mental and emotional well-being, secure values and belief, ambition and able to relate to others and manage themselves, pursue a healthy and active lifestyle, be self-aware, develop and communicate their own beliefs and view of the world, life as independently as they can, assess risk and take informed decisions, achieve success in different areas of activity • Responsible citizens with respect for others, commitment to participate responsibly in political, economic, social and cultural life a and able to develop knowledge and understanding of the world and Scotland's place in it, understand different beliefs and cultures, make informed choices and decisions, evaluate environmental, scientific and technological issues, develop informed, ethical views and complex issues • Effective contributors with an enterprising attitude, resilience, self-reliance, and able to communicate in different ways and in different settings, work in partnership and in teams, take the initiative and lead, apply critical thinking in new contexts, create and develop, solve problems
Sweden	Norms and values: • can consciously determine and express ethical standpoints based on knowledge of human rights and basic democratic values, as well as personal experiences • respects the intrinsic value of other people • rejects the subjection of people to oppression and degrading treatment, and also assists in helping other people • can empathise with and understand the situation other people are in and also develop the will to act with their best interests at heart • shows respect and care for both the immediate environment, as well as the environment from a broader perspective. Knowledge: • can use the Swedish language, both in speech and writing, in a rich and varied way • can communicate in English, both in spoken and written language, and also be given opportunities to communicate in some other foreign language in a functional way • can use mathematical reasoning for further studies and in everyday life • can use knowledge from scientific, technical, social science, humanistic and aesthetic areas of knowledge for further studies, in societal and everyday life • can solve problems and transform ideas into action in a creative way • can learn, research, and work independently and together with others, and feel confident in their own ability • can make use of critical thinking and independently formulate standpoints based on knowledge and ethical considerations • has obtained knowledge about and insight into the Swedish, Nordic and Western cultural heritage, and also obtained basic knowledge of the Nordic languages • has obtained knowledge about the cultures, languages, religion and history of the national minorities (Jews, Romanies, indigenous Samis, Swedish and Tornedal Finns) • can interact with other people based on knowledge of similarities and differences in living conditions, culture, language, religion and history

Source: (OECD, 2021[2]) *Future of Education and Skills 2030, Policy Questionnaire on Curriculum Redesign (PQC)* (2021), item 1.1.2. https://www.oecd.org/education/2030-project/curriculum-analysis/data/.

Table 1.1[8/8] **Educational goals and criteria for success in ISTP jurisdictions**

	Country/jurisdiction	Student profile
OECD	Sweden	<ul><li>has obtained knowledge of society's laws and norms, human rights and democratic values in school and in society</li><li>has obtained knowledge about the prerequisites for a good environment and sustainable development</li><li>has obtained knowledge about and an understanding of the importance of the individual's own lifestyle and its impact on health, the environment and society</li><li>can use and understand many different forms of expression such as language, art, music, drama and dance, and also has developed an awareness of the range of culture existing in society</li><li>can use modern technology as a tool in the search for knowledge, communication, creativity and learning</li><li>can make well-informed choices regarding further education and vocational orientation</li></ul>
Partners	China (People's Republic of)	<ul><li>spirit of patriotism, collectivism, love of socialism, inherit and develop the splendid Chinese traditional culture and revolutionary spirit</li><li>a healthy body and psychological quality, and a healthy aesthetic value and lifestyle to become a new generation with lofty ideals, moral integrity, better education</li><li>good sense of discipline</li><li>at the social level: socialist legal awareness should abide by national law and social morality, gradually form correct outlook on world, life and values, form a sense of social responsibility to serve the people</li><li>at the personal level: basic spirit of innovation, ability of practice, scientific quality, humanistic literacy, awareness of environmental protection, basic knowledge, skills and methods for lifelong learning</li></ul>
	Hong Kong (China)	<ul><li>all-round development according to his/her own attributes in the domains of ethics, intellect, physique, social skills, aesthetics</li><li>capable of lifelong learning, critical and exploratory thinking, innovating and adapting to change, filled with self-confidence, a team spirit, willing to put forward continuing effort for the prosperity, progress, freedom and democracy of their society, contribute to the future well-being of the nation and the world at large</li></ul>
	Singapore	<ul><li>Has a good sense of self-awareness</li><li>Has a sound moral compass</li><li>Has the necessary skills and knowledge to take on challenges of the future</li><li>Is responsible to his/her family, community and nation</li><li>Appreciates the beauty of the surrounding world</li><li>Possesses a healthy mind and body</li><li>Has a zest for life</li><li>A confident person who has a strong sense of right and wrong, is adaptable and resilient, knows him/herself, is discerning in judgment, thinks independently and critically, and communicates effectively</li><li>A self-directed learner who takes responsibility for his/her own learning, who questions, reflects and perseveres in the pursuit of learning</li><li>An active contributor who is able to work effectively on teams, exercises initiative, takes calculated risks, is innovative and strives for excellence</li><li>A concerned citizen who is rooted in Singapore, has a strong civic consciousness, is informed, and takes an active role in bettering the lives of others around him/her</li></ul>

Source: (OECD, 2021[2]) *Future of Education and Skills 2030, Policy Questionnaire on Curriculum Redesign (PQC)* (2021), item 1.1.2. https://www.oecd.org/education/2030-project/curriculum-analysis/data/.

COLLABORATIVE STRATEGIES TO IMPLEMENT NEW EDUCATIONAL GOALS

The process of establishing learning goals can be as important as the product. The road of curriculum design and implementation is littered with many good ideas that were poorly implemented.

The laws, regulations, structures and institutions on which educational goals and curricula are established are just the small visible tip of the iceberg. The reason why it is so hard to advance implementation is that there is a much larger invisible part under the waterline. This invisible part is composed of the interests, beliefs, motivations and fears of those involved in education, teachers included. This is where unexpected collisions occur because this part of educational reform is rarely captured on the radar screen of public policy. Policy makers reform education successfully when they help people recognise what needs to change and build a shared understanding and collective ownership for change. They must focus resources, build capacity, and create the right policy climate with accountability measures designed to encourage innovation and development rather than compliance.

Because of education systems' vast structure of established providers and extensive vested interests, reform is often accompanied by loss of advantages or privileged positions. Furthermore, parents often become anxious that their children are no longer learning things that were important to them, or when their children learn things they themselves as parents no longer understand. As a result, the status quo has many protectors – stakeholders in education who stand or perceive to lose if changes are made. Add to this the asymmetry between the costs and benefits of change: costs are immediate and certain while there is uncertainty about who will benefit from change.

Not least, while the road to successfully implementing new learning goals is a long one, failure is often just one small step away. Curriculum reform easily becomes a thankless task when elections take place before the benefits of reform are realised. Ministers can lose their post in an election over education issues when something goes wrong but education issues will rarely win an election because it takes so much time to translate good ideas into better outcomes.

Working together for successful reform

At the same time, there has been important progress in this field in the last few years. While governments and teacher organisations often sit at opposite sides of the negotiation table, they are increasingly coming together over the vision and design of the education system and related learning goals. Often this includes public consultations or discussions on educational goals or curricula (see Box 1.1 for a more detailed description of selected approaches).

Engaging key stakeholders, especially teachers, in envisioning desired student outcomes is key to making the vision a reality. Properly designed stakeholder engagement helps ensure that the voices of learners, educators, parents and communities are heard on society's future needs. This builds capacity for curriculum implementation more efficiently. When stakeholders strongly buy into the vision they have sketched out together, it can become a powerful tool to inspire schools, communities, and the education system to achieve the desired outcomes for all learners.

In 2017, Portugal produced its Student Profile. The profile was guided by a vision, values and principles – all of which were crafted in collaboration between key stakeholders. Expert consultation, meetings with teachers, administrators and parents all provided crucial information and created stakeholder support. This process involved students themselves – from the youngest ages. The Student Profile outlines actions for teachers and the commitment that should be made by schools and cultivated among families and parents. Portugal also engaged in a deliberate approach to communicate about the Student Profile. This included 'Student Profile Day', which was well covered with live streaming to every school in the country. ARtv media partner ensured that the event would be broadcast for viewing by the broader population. The broad and popular base of the panel involved on the day (a prominent Portuguese TV presenter, the national football team's coach, a well-known judge, a scientist, a journalist and a young pop star) gave the event freshness and relevance (for more examples, see Box 1.1).

Strategic foresight, careful planning and consultative and collaborative processes take time but they contribute to more sustainable and successful results. OECD's Education 2030 project offers the following five lessons for successful stakeholder engagement in the setting of learning goals and curriculum implementation.

Do not underestimate teachers' fear of the unknown and allow them space for mistakes

Setting learning goals that go beyond current practice can be met with resistance from stakeholders. Resistance to change may be especially strong among teachers when the nature of the change is unfamiliar (e.g. new concepts and use of new educational technologies) and the consequences on their teaching are unclear. Wanting innovation in the classroom requires everyone to allow mistakes and see them as steps towards better schools.

Several jurisdictions in OECD's Education 2030 programme report that a lack of teacher buy-in for curriculum reform, manifesting as scepticism or doubt about reform (as in Korea and Poland), fear of change (as in Ireland), and personal beliefs or attitudes that conflict with a new curricular direction (as in Singapore) can present barriers to effective and timely curriculum implementation. Singapore notes the difficulty of getting teachers ready for the implementation of the revised curriculum to ensure that classroom practices do not deviate from the intent of the syllabi and curriculum. Implementation can be impeded by teachers' attitudes and beliefs on the subject, their own teaching styles and practices and also by a lack of lead time for teachers to acquaint themselves with the revised curriculum.

Such resistance is often due to a fear of the unknown, with teachers reporting being ill-equipped for such change. Teacher training programmes and guidance materials can also be misaligned with new curriculum directions, adding to resistance. Teachers especially fear making mistakes in implementing the new curriculum. This can mean that they continue to teach in a traditional way and students potentially miss out on opportunities to develop future-oriented skills.

Awareness-raising campaigns and inspirational leadership can help motivate teachers for change. Teachers also need to be reassured that the goal of change is attainable and that sufficient support (training, guidance and materials) will be provided throughout the implementation process. This can ultimately increase teacher agency, ensure their well-being and contribute to a sense of accomplishment. Some jurisdictions also reported positive experiences with teacher learning communities, where challenges are discovered collectively.

Empower, not disempower, teachers with digital technologies

The use of digital technologies can make learning more granular, more adaptive, and more interactive. Digital technologies also enable content, pedagogies and assessments to be better integrated. For example, when digital learning environments facilitate learning, they can also provide positive feedback that helps teachers detect biases. Learning analytics can help teachers manage their classes both in real time during teaching and as a reflective tool afterwards by supporting professional learning and suggesting solutions to ensure better student engagement.

However, technology can also contribute to some teachers surrendering decisions regarding curriculum content, pedagogies and assessments to technology. This can then create dependence and diminish teachers' agency. The best answer to this is to engage teachers in the design of such digital solutions rather than confront them with implementation.

Reconcile incremental changes to the curriculum with maintaining aspirations for transformational change

While acknowledging that transformational change is essential to keep curriculum content relevant to social demands, jurisdictions reported that there are significant challenges involved in "getting it right". Some jurisdictions surveyed by the Education 2030 project resorted to less burdensome incremental changes by revising curriculum/guidelines partially and on demand. This emphasises the importance of "small wins" in reform implementation. Others create space in the curriculum from the onset to accommodate new changes rapidly, for instance, by setting up a dedicated subject for cross-curriculum content. However, jurisdictions have also reported that incremental changes often result in a patchwork curriculum with possible time lags before achieving tangible impact. Creating space in the curriculum should also be handled with caution so as not to provoke curriculum overload by adding more instruction time and/or creating incoherence across grades and learning areas.

Maintaining a balance between a transformational whole-system change and speedier "on demand" incremental changes keeps curriculum reforms moving forward in a meaningful and efficient manner, and contains the time lag while gradually incorporating the competencies and skills needed for the future.

Avoid reform fatigue among stakeholders by designing synergies between curriculum change and other educational reforms

Reform fatigue resulting from too-frequent changes and adjustments to learning goals and curricula often leads to stakeholders becoming less engaged over time. It also builds up resistance to change in the long run. Reform fatigue may be particularly pertinent if curriculum and/or pedagogical changes are implemented before previous reforms have been embedded into practice, or if teachers are faced with contradictory reforms in a relatively short period of time.

Jurisdictions in OECD's Education 2030 programme reported being confronted with teachers ignoring reforms, just doing the minimum, or reinforcing old processes, methods and content. However, when opting for more continuity and stability (i.e. regular cyclical curriculum reforms instead of periodical curriculum renewals), they found that curriculum change was insufficiently responsive to the pace of change in society.

It takes time to build trust in changes and policy reforms. It is important to support the process through awareness-raising campaigns and synergies with other successful reforms or reform initiatives. Rebuilding trust is even more critical in the event of a series of reforms, especially if they have not fully succeeded.

Capitalise on the opportunities of technology for the design of curricula and learning environments while being aware of cyber security threats and personal data issues

The shift towards digital/e curricula can be an efficient solution to reduce cost and time associated with curriculum redesign. This is especially so because it eliminates the back and forth of printing and reprinting hard copies when changes are made. A digital curriculum substantially reduces costs and makes it possible to adjust curriculum content as needed in an iterative manner as well as to give teachers greater agency in how they engage with the content.

However, one unintended consequence reported by jurisdictions is that the more easily amendable format can lead to frequent alterations by curriculum developers and e curriculum managers. This is very frustrating for teachers as they are exposed to constant adjustments with additional, altered or superseded content, contributing to reform fatigue.

Caution is also necessary when modernising curriculum content to keep up with new societal developments. Given how quickly views and values in society change, the curriculum can easily end up with redundant references to specific issues, events and tools. To avoid this, it is crucial for curriculum to focus on core concepts that are valued in each discipline or across disciplines, as well as on key concepts that endure over time.

A degree of discipline is, therefore, required on the part of those responsible for digital curriculum adjustments, focusing on fundamentally important adjustments rather than small scale cosmetic changes. Otherwise, teachers, parents, and students may be frustrated by constant and confusing changes. With a shift to a digital curriculum, there is also a need to invest in stronger cybersecurity, not only tackling the technological security aspects of the hardware and software used, but building a culture of security among the end-users of the digital space (teachers, students, principals and parents).

Box 1.1 Examples of students profiles and learning goals

Portugal: The **Students' Profile by the End of Compulsory Schooling** is structured in principles, vision, values and competence areas that all students should develop by the end of 12 years of education. The values outlined in the profile's conceptual framework mirror the humanistic philosophy of inclusion and values diversity whereby each student is viewed as a unique human being. The students' profile leads thus to a school education in which the students of this global generation build and settle a humanistic scientific and artistic culture by mobilising values and skills that allow them to act upon the life and history of individuals and societies; to make free and informed decisions about natural, social and ethical issues; and to carry out civic, active, conscious and responsible participation (Portuguese Ministry of Education, 2017[2]).

Korea: Based on the Korean concept of "**Hongik Ingan**", or the drive to broadly benefit humanity, Korea sets out its student profile, "**An Educated Person**". It aims to enable every citizen to lead a life worthy of human dignity, contribute to the development of a democratic state and support the realisation of an ideal of shared human prosperity by ensuring cultivation of character, development of abilities for independent life and necessary qualities as a democratic citizen under the humanitarian ideal. Based on the ideal and aims of education, the vision of an educated person in this curriculum is specified as follows: 1) a self-directed person who builds a self-identity and explores a career and life on the basis of holistic growth; 2) a creative person who discovers something novel by means of diverse ideas and challenges based upon basic abilities; 3) a cultivated person who appreciates and promotes the culture of humankind on the basis of cultural literacy and understanding of diverse values; and 4) a person who lives in harmony with others, fulfilling the ethics of caring and sharing, as a democratic citizen with a sense of community and connection to the world.

| Infographic 1.1 | **Portugal's students' profile by the end of compulsory schooling** |

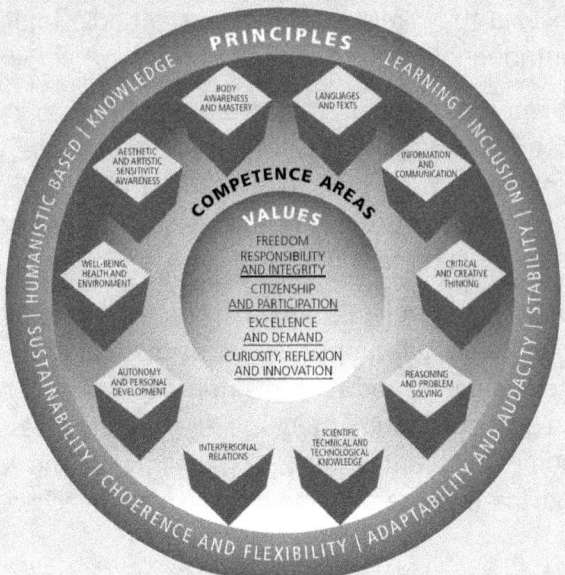

Note: For more details see "What Students Learn Matters: Towards a 21st Century Curriculum" and Annex on National or regional curriculum frameworks and visualisations.
Source: Students' Profile by the End of Compulsory Schooling, Directorate-General for Education/Ministry of Education and Science (2017) from (OECD, 2020[4]), *What Students Learn Matters: Towards a 21st Century Curriculum*, OECD Publishing, Paris, https://doi.org/10.1787/d86d4d9a-en, p. 74.

| Infographic 1.2 | **Student profile Korea** |

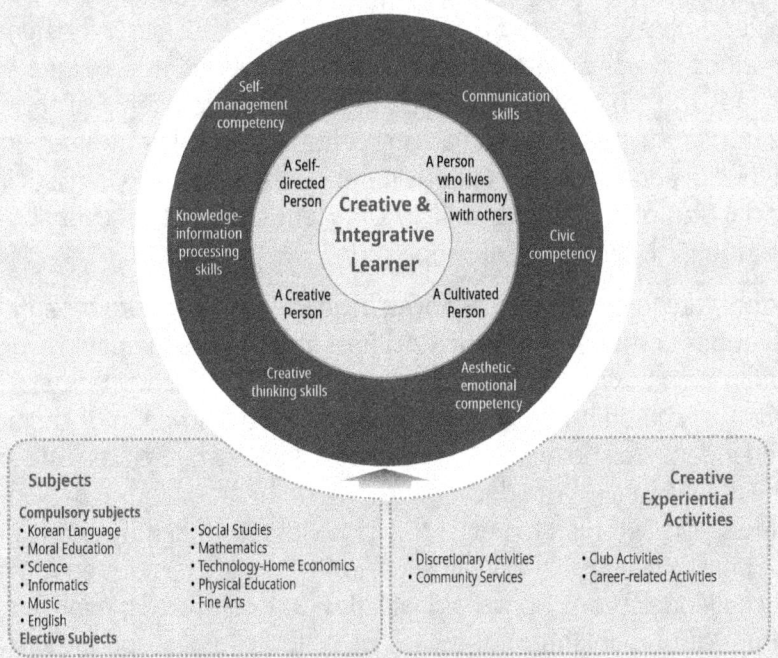

The Framework for 2015 Revised Middle School Curriculum in Korea

Note: For more details see "What Students Learn Matters: Towards a 21st Century Curriculum" and Annex on National or regional curriculum frameworks and visualisations.
Source: (Korea Institute for Curriculum and Evaluation, 2016[5]), The Framework for 2015 Revised Middle School Curriculum in Korea from (OECD, 2020[4]), *What Students Learn Matters: Towards a 21st Century Curriculum*, OECD Publishing, Paris, https://doi.org/10.1787/d86d4d9a-en, p. 75.

Scotland (United Kingdom): Scotland (United Kingdom) defines its student profile based on four main dimensions to be enabled among young people: 1) successful learners; 2) confident individuals; 3) responsible citizens; and 4) effective contributors. Under each of these dimensions, Scotland includes values and competencies that support students to navigate towards such a vision. This student profile helps to align values and competencies with education objectives under a clear and coherent framework that sets out a broad reference of the Scottish curriculum for students, teachers and stakeholders.

Infographic 1.3 Student profile Scotland (United Kingdom)

A curriculum framework to meet the needs of all learners 3 – 18
A schematic guide for curriculum planners

Values
Wisdom, justice, compassion, integrity

The curriculum must be inclusive, be a stimulus for personal achievement and, through the broadening of experience of the world, be an encouragement towards informed and responsible citizenship.

The curriculum: 'the totality of all that is planned for children and young people throughout their education'
- Ethos and life of the school as a community
- Curriculum areas and subjects
- Interdisciplinary learning
- Opportunities for personal achievement

Learning and teaching
- Engaging and active
- Setting challenging goals
- Shared expectations and standards
- Timely, accurate feedback
- Learning intentions, success criteria, personal learning planning
- Collaborative
- Reflecting the ways different learners progress

Experiences and outcomes set out expectations for learning and development in:
- Expressive arts
- Languages and literacy
- Health and wellbeing
- Mathematics and numeracy
- Religious and moral education
- Sciences
- Social studies
- Technologies

Curriculum levels describe progression and development.

[Central diagram: Learner at centre, surrounded by outcomes and experiences, framed by literacy, numeracy, health & wellbeing, and the four capacities: successful learners, confident individuals, responsible citizens, effective contributors, with skills for learning, skills for life and skills for work]

All children and young people are entitled to experience
- a coherent curriculum from 3 to 18
- a broad general education, including well planned experiences and outcomes across all the curriculum areas. This should include understanding of the world and Scotland's place in it and understanding of the environment
- a senior phase which provides opportunities for study for qualifications and other planned opportunities for developing the four capacities
- opportunities for developing skills for learning, skills for life and skills for work
- opportunities to achieve to the highest levels they can through appropriate personal support and challenge
- Opportunities to move into positive and sustained destinations beyond school

Personal Support
- review of learning and planning of next steps
- gaining access to learning activities which will meet their needs
- planning for opportunities for personal achievement
- preparing for changes and choices and support through changes and choices
- pre-school centres and schools working with partners

Principles for curriculum design:
- Challenge and enjoyment
- Breadth
- Progression
- Depth
- Personalisation and choice
- Coherence
- Relevance

Arrangements for
- Assessment
- Qualifications
- Self-evaluation and accountability
- Professional development

to support the purposes of learning

Note: For more details see "What Students Learn Matters: Towards a 21st Century Curriculum" and Annex on National or regional curriculum frameworks and visualisations.
Source: Education Analysis Division – The Scottish Government 2017 from (OECD, 2020[4]), What Students Learn Matters: Towards a 21st Century Curriculum, OECD Publishing, Paris, https://doi.org/10.1787/d86d4d9a-en, p. 75.

Hong Kong (China): Hong Kong (China) has a set of 7 Learning Goals which describe the aim of its student profile. On a secondary education level, it aims to enable students to: 1) become an informed and responsible citizen with a sense of national and global identity, appreciation of positive values and attitudes as well as Chinese culture, and respect for pluralism in society; 2) acquire and construct a broad and solid knowledge base, and to understand contemporary issues that may impact on students' daily lives at personal, community, national and global levels; 3) become proficient in bi-literate and trilingual communication for better study and life; 4) develop and apply generic skills in an integrative manner, and to become an independent and self-directed learner for future study and work; 5) use information and information technology ethically, flexibly and effectively; 6) understand one's own interests, aptitudes and abilities, and to develop and reflect upon personal goals with aspirations for further studies and future career; and 7) lead a healthy lifestyle with active participation in physical and aesthetic activities, and to appreciate sports and the arts.

Infographic 1.4 Hong Kong (China) learning goals

Note: For more details see "What Students Learn Matters: Towards a 21st Century Curriculum" and Annex on National or regional curriculum frameworks and visualisations.
Source: Curriculum Development Council (2017), Learning Goals, School Curriculum Framework and Planning, *Secondary Education Curriculum Guide*, Figure 2.2, https://www.edb.gov.hk/attachment/en/curriculum-development/renewal/Guides/SECG_booklet_2_en_20180831.pdf from (OECD, 2020[4]), *What Students Learn Matters: Towards a 21st Century Curriculum*, OECD Publishing, Paris, https://doi.org/10.1787/d86d4d9a-en, p. 76.

Council of Ministers of Education, Canada (CMEC): In 2016, the provincial and territorial ministers of Education put forward six global competencies in a pan-Canadian effort to prepare students for a complex and unpredictable future with rapidly changing political, social, economic, technological, and ecological landscapes. Building on strong foundations of numeracy and literacy, these competencies are: Critical Thinking and Problem Solving; Innovation, Creativity, and Entrepreneurship; Learning to Learn/ Self-Awareness and Self-Direction; Collaboration; Communication; and Global Citizenship and Sustainability. These competencies are an overarching set of attitudes, skills, knowledge and values that are interdependent, interdisciplinary, and can be leveraged in a variety of situations both locally and globally. They provide learners with the abilities to meet the shifting and ongoing demands of life, work and learning; to be active and responsive in their communities; to understand diverse perspectives; and to act on issues of global significance. This framework is closely aligned with the competencies that have been prioritised through the introduction of new curricula, programmes, and initiatives. It is anticipated to evolve based on provincial and territorial engagement with these competencies.

> Infographic 1.5 — The Council of Ministers of Education, Canada's (CMEC) pan-Canadian global competencies

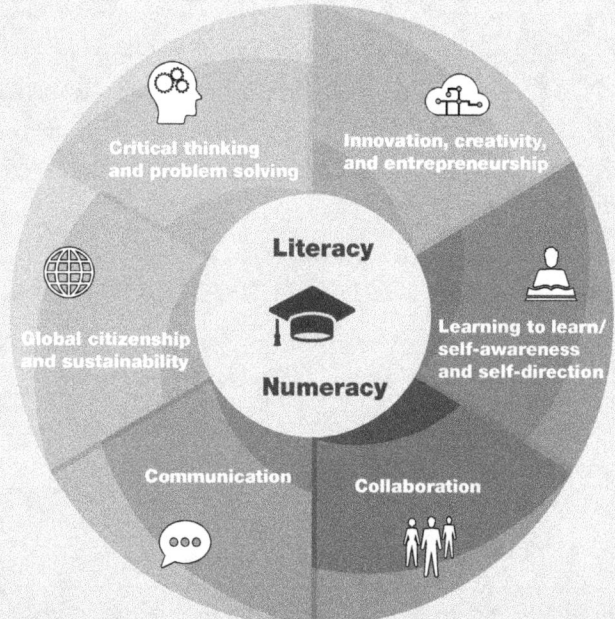

Note: For more details see "What Students Learn Matters: Towards a 21st Century Curriculum" and Annex on National or regional curriculum frameworks and visualisations.
Sources: (Council of Ministers of Education, Canada (2020), *Pan-Canadian Global Competencies*, https://static1.squarespace.com/static/5af1e87f5cfd79c163407ead/t/5c6597f353450a15233b6e7c/1550161912721/Pan-Canadian+Global+Competencies+Backgrounder_EN.pdf from (OECD, 2020[4]), *What Students Learn Matters: Towards a 21st Century Curriculum*, OECD Publishing, Paris, https://doi.org/10.1787/d86d4d9a-en, p.76.

REFERENCES

Korea Institute for Curriculum and Evaluation (2016), *The Framework for 2015 Revised Middle School Curriculum in Korea,* unpublished manuscript. [5]

OECD (2021), *Future of Education and Skills 2030, Policy Questionnaire on Curriculum Redesign (PQC),* OECD Publishing, Paris, https://www.oecd.org/education/2030-project/curriculum-analysis/data/. [2]

OECD (2020), *What Students Learn Matters: Towards a 21st Century Curriculum,* OECD Publishing, Paris, https://doi.org/10.1787/d86d4d9a-en. [4]

Portuguese Ministry of Education (2017), *Perfil dos Alunos a Saida sa Escolaridade Obrigatoria,* https://www.dge.mec.pt/noticias/perfil-dos-alunos-saida-da-escolaridade-obrigatoria. [3]

02
SUPPORTING THE WHOLE CHILD

Building on child development and learning sciences research, what is needed to support each person's learning (including academic knowledge) with mental and physical health, and social emotional learning?

The well-being of students, teachers and other critical educators are precursors to improving education. How does the teaching profession best support student well-being? How do we value and support the teaching profession and support the well-being of teachers? What support do teachers need, including collaboration with other educators (such as support personnel) and other professions in enhancing student well-being and mental health?

Supporting the whole child

If parents are asked what they want for their children, many mention "achievement" or "success" but many also reply "happiness", "confidence", "resilience", "kindness", "health", "satisfaction", and the like. In short, people value the development of the whole child and the pandemic has heightened focus on this.

Children spend a considerable amount of time in the classroom – following lessons, socialising with classmates, and interacting with teachers and other staff members. By the time they enter school, children differ in how easily and intensely they become anxious, frustrated or positively excited. They also differ in capacities for attention and self-regulation. Children's temperament, self-regulation and capacity for attention continue to develop throughout the school years. Experiences of success and failure during a child's adjustment to the challenges of school influence the child's representations and evaluations of self, peers and adults. What happens in school is key to understanding whether students enjoy good physical and mental health, how happy and satisfied they are with different aspects of their life, how connected to others they feel, and the aspirations they have for their future.

Teachers are powerful figures in the lives of most children. A positive class atmosphere where efforts are encouraged and rewarded and in which children are accepted and supported by their teachers, regardless of their intellect and temperament, is often associated with more positive reactions to the demands of schooling, and to lower school-related stress. Even the most vulnerable child has capacities for positive experiences at school. "Accentuating the positive" in the child's experience of school can serve to increase autonomy, motivation and resilience, essential qualities for success both in and outside of school.

STRENGTHENING STUDENT RESILIENCE AND AGENCY

Students who were able to learn independently, to set their own learning goals, to adjust their learning strategies, and to cope with adversity and failure had a huge advantage during the pandemic. This advantage will remain relevant in the more open and flexible learning environments of the future, and it will certainly be key to the willingness and capacity of people to continue learning throughout their lives.

To capture this, the PISA 2018 assessment added an important new perspective to educational outcomes: student agency – the capacity to set goals, reflect and act responsibly to effect change. The concept of agency is rooted in the belief that students need to develop the ability and the will to positively influence their own lives and the world around them.

Environmental issues offer a good illustration of how student awareness, knowledge and agency can be at odds.

When it comes to environmental awareness, 79% of students across OECD countries said in PISA 2018 they knew about the topic of climate change and global warming, a figure that ranged, when considering all 66 countries covered by this PISA survey, from 40% in Saudi Arabia to around 90% in Hong Kong (China) and Singapore (see left panel in Figure 2). In most countries, the majority of students also reported fairly high levels of self-efficacy when it comes to environmental issues. For example, an average of 72% of students said they could easily or, at least, with some effort explain why some countries suffer more from global climate change than others; 65% said they could discuss the consequences of economic development on the environment; and 63% said they could explain how carbon dioxide emissions affect global climate change.

These fairly high percentages are not surprising when considering that 88% of school principals reported that global warming and climate change were covered in the school curriculum, a percentage that exceeded 50% in all of the 66 countries except Israel and 75% in all but 12 countries.

The high level of student awareness should also be seen in the context of how much the environment matters to most young people: an average of 78% of students in OECD countries agreed or strongly agreed with the statement that "looking after the global environment is important to me". In no country did this figure fall below 64%.

However, when students were asked whether they could do something about global problems like climate change, the figure dropped to an average of 57% (see right panel in Figure 2.1). In Germany, the Slovak Republic, Romania, Hungary, Latvia, Moldova, Russia, Austria, Switzerland, Malaysia, Slovenia, Serbia, Belarus and Estonia, the percentage fell to less than half. And, when asked whether they think their behaviour can impact people in other countries, the average figure dropped further, to 44%. Interestingly, PISA top performers Korea and Singapore showed, with 20% and 24% respectively, some of the lowest shares of students who are confident they can have a global impact.

So, while students show a high level of awareness and interest in the future of the planet and, to some extent, take responsibility for this in their daily lives, they do not feel a sense of empowerment and agency to make a real difference. The same discrepancy between awareness and agency became apparent for other global challenges that PISA 2018 surveyed too. This does not necessarily reflect a lack of attention to those issues in school; as noted above, school principals in most countries say that climate change now features at least in some form in their curricula. But it suggests that students do not experience a sense of being in control that gives them the capacity to positively influence their own life and the world around them.

Schools need to do better in helping students develop a sense of self-efficacy, agency and responsibility. Only in this way can young people unleash their knowledge and energy to build sustainable cities, start sustainable businesses, push the innovation frontier for green technologies, rethink individual lifestyles, back ecologically responsible policy making, and, most importantly, strike the right balance between meeting the needs of the present and safeguarding the ability of future generations to meet their own needs.

These issues can be addressed. OECD's Education 2030 Learning Compass has identified many examples in which student agency is successfully developed and exercised in different contexts, whether social, economic, creative or moral.

STUDENT WELL-BEING – AND WHAT TEACHERS AND PARENTS CAN DO TO FOSTER IT

While the well-being of students has always been part of school curricula, the pandemic has given this aspect an entirely new dimension. PISA is offering an international comparative perspective on this. The strength of PISA here is that it is possible to study the interrelationships between student well-being and other educational outcomes together with important individual, institutional and systemic factors and agents related to these, teachers included. Unless otherwise noted, results in this section refer to the PISA 2018 assessment.

Figure 2.1 Young people care about climate change but feel unable to make a difference

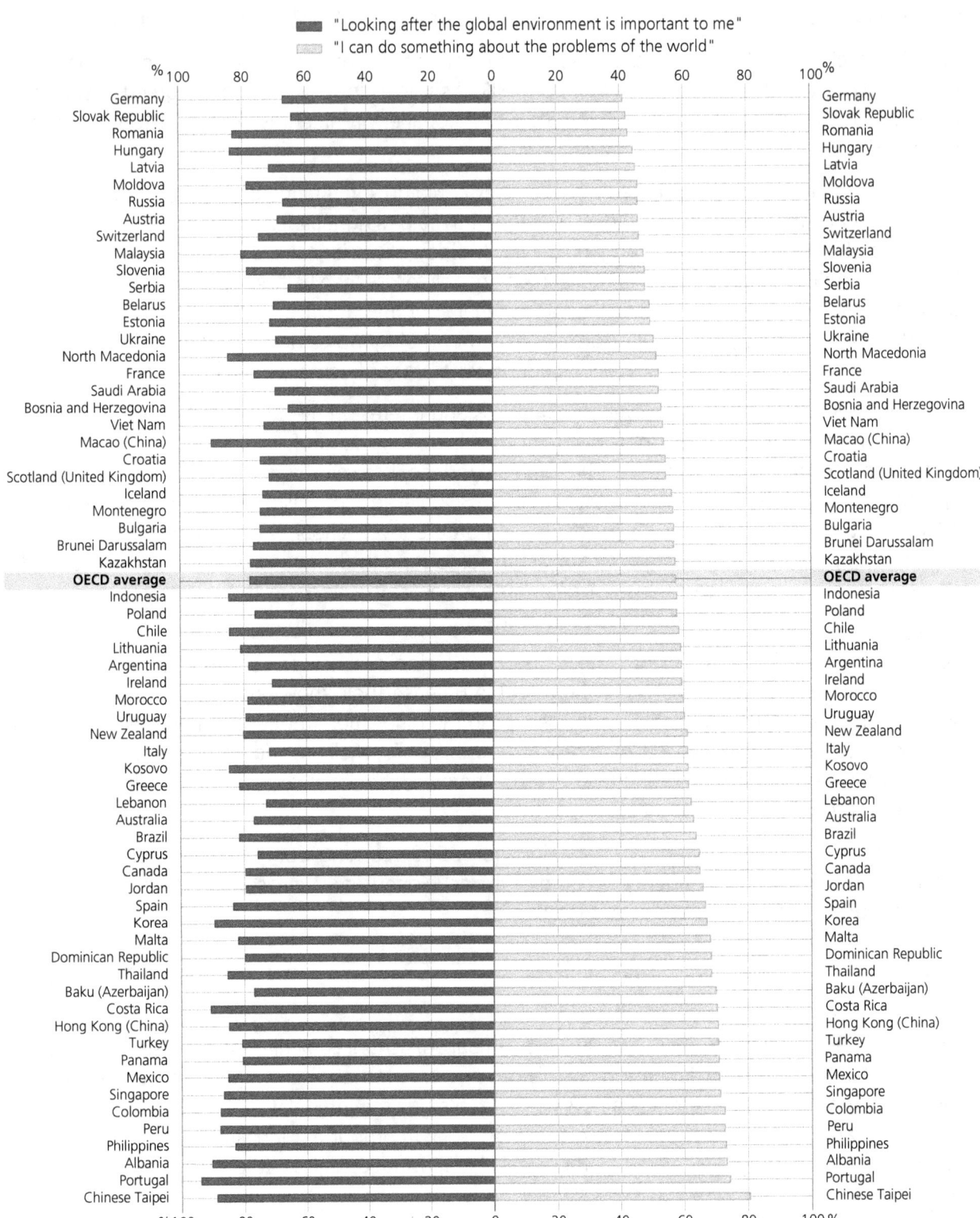

Source: Adapted from (OECD, 2020[6]), *PISA 2018 Results (Volume VI): Are Students Ready to Thrive in an Interconnected World?*, PISA, OECD Publishing, Paris, https://doi.org/10.1787/d5f68679-en, Table VI.B1.5.1 Agency regarding global issue https://doi.org/10.1787/888934171210.

As Figure 2.2 illustrates, students' well-being is the result of interactions among four interrelated domains: cognitive, psychological, social and physical. Each dimension can be considered both as an outcome and as an enabling condition with respect to the other dimensions, and ultimately with students' overall quality of life.

- The cognitive dimension of students' well-being refers to the cognitive foundations students need to participate fully in today's society, as lifelong learners, effective workers and engaged citizens. In PISA cognitive well-being is primarily measured through assessments of learning outcomes.

- The psychological dimension of students' well-being includes students' sense of purpose in life, self-awareness, affective states and emotional strength. Psychological well-being is supported by self-esteem, motivation, resilience, self-efficacy, hope and optimism; it is hindered by anxiety, stress, depression and distorted views of the self and others. PISA measures some aspects of psychological well-being through students' reports of their motivation for achievement and schoolwork-related anxiety.

- The social dimension of students' well-being refers to the quality of their social lives. It includes students' relationships with their family, their peers and their teachers, and students' feelings about their social life in and outside of school. PISA measures students' sense of belonging at school. The quality of students' social relationships at school is also measured through students' self-reported exposure to bullying and perceptions of teachers' fairness.

- The physical dimension of students' well-being refers to students' health and the adoption of a healthy lifestyle. PISA provides self-reported information on how much physical activity students engage in and on whether they eat regularly.

Figure 2.2 A framework for student well-being

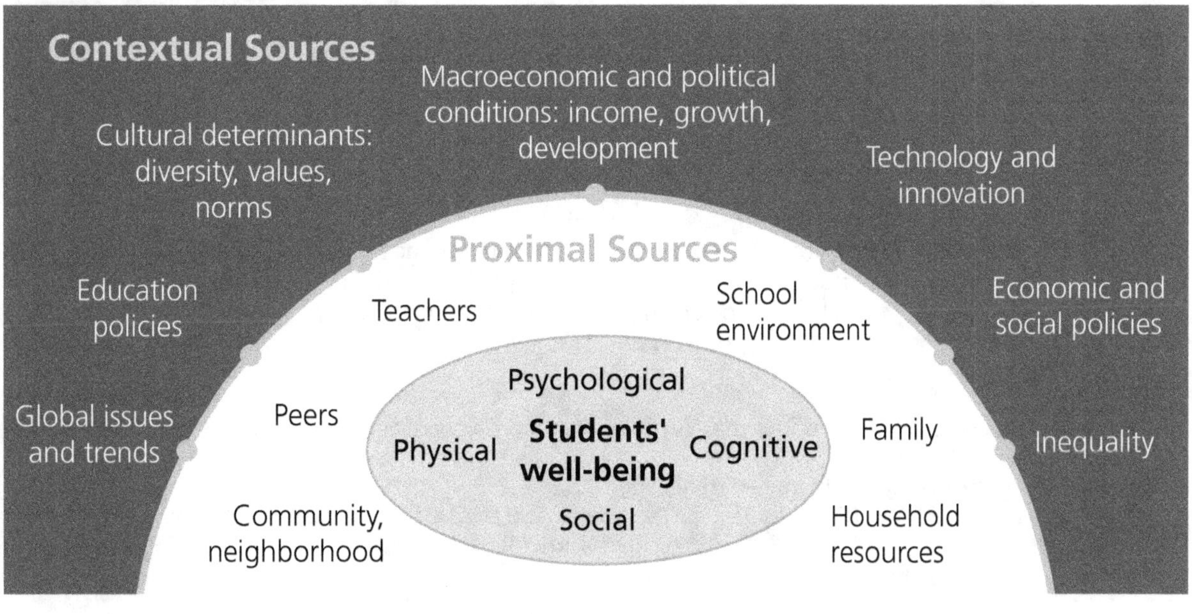

Contextual Sources

- Cultural determinants: diversity, values, norms
- Macroeconomic and political conditions: income, growth, development
- Technology and innovation
- Education policies
- Economic and social policies
- Global issues and trends
- Inequality

Proximal Sources

- Teachers
- School environment
- Peers
- Family
- Community, neighborhood
- Household resources

Students' well-being: Psychological, Physical, Cognitive, Social

Source: (OECD, 2017[7]), *PISA 2015 Results (Volume III): Students' Well-Being*, PISA, OECD Publishing, Paris, http://dx.doi.org/10.1787/9789264273856-en, Figure III.2.2, https://doi.org/10.1787/19963777.

On average across OECD countries, 67% of students reported being satisfied with their lives (students who reported between 7 and 10 on the PISA life-satisfaction scale). Some 68% of students across OECD countries agreed that their life has clear meaning or purpose. However, between 2015 and 2018, the share of students satisfied with their lives shrank by 5 percentage points on average across OECD countries.

There is considerable variation within countries: girls and disadvantaged students were less likely to report being satisfied with their lives than boys and advantaged students, respectively. Students with the least exposure to bullying reported an average of 7.5 on the 10-point life-satisfaction scale; students with the greatest exposure to bullying averaged 6.3 on the scale (Figure 2.3). PISA learning outcomes were higher among students who reported they are "somehow satisfied" and "moderately satisfied" with their lives and lower among students who reported they are "not satisfied" or "very satisfied" with their lives.

Figure 2.3 Student life satisfaction and its relationship with school factors (OECD average)

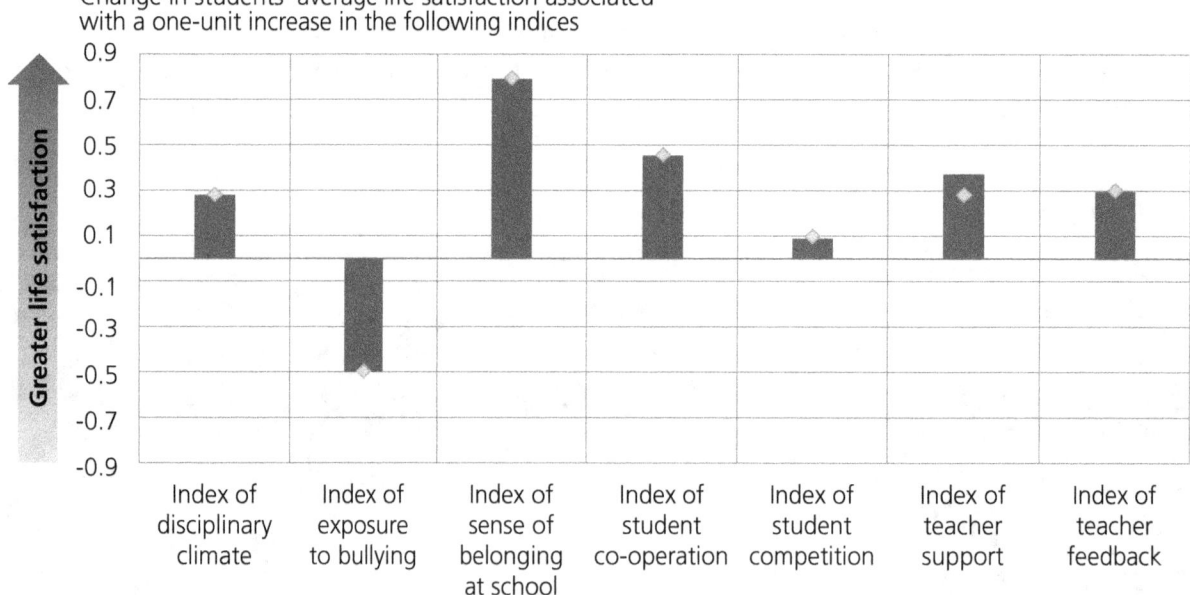

1. Student and school characteristics include the PISA index of economic, social and cultural status (ESCS) at the student and school levels and gender.
Note: All values are statistically significant (see Annex A3).
Source: (OECD, 2019[8]), *PISA 2018 Results (Volume III): What School Life Means for Students' Lives,* PISA, OECD Publishing, Paris, https://doi.org/10.1787/acd78851-en Table III.B1.11.10, http://dx.doi.org/10.1787/888934031047.

Across OECD countries, the majority of students reported that they feel socially connected at school (Figure 2.4). For instance, three out of four students agreed or strongly agreed that they can make friends easily at school. The majority of students in all countries that participated in PISA reported that they feel they belong to the school community. However, also here in the vast majority of countries, students' sense of belonging at school has weakened since 2003. Students who reported that they feel like outsiders at school were, on average across OECD countries, about three times more likely to be unsatisfied with their lives compared with students who did not report so. Students who reported that they feel like outsiders scored 22 points lower in PISA than students who did not report so.

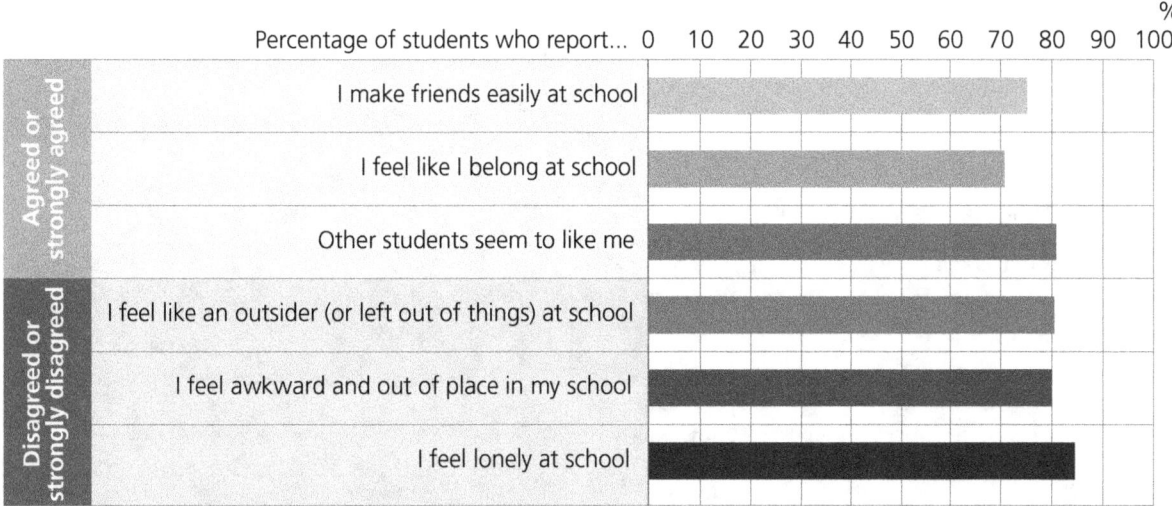

Figure 2.4 Student sense of belonging

Source: (OECD, 2019[8]), *PISA 2018 Results (Volume III): What School Life Means for Students' Lives*, PISA, OECD Publishing, Paris, https://doi.org/10.1787/acd78851-en Table III.B1.9.1, http://dx.doi.org/10.1787/888934031009.

On average across OECD countries, students who reported a greater sense of belonging scored higher in the PISA reading assessment after accounting for socio-economic status. Students reported a greater sense of belonging when they also reported higher levels of co-operation among their peers, whereas students' perception of competition was not associated with their sense of belonging at school. Students who reported a greater sense of belonging were also more likely to expect to complete a university degree even after accounting for socio-economic status, gender, immigrant background and overall reading performance.

In sum, the results from PISA show that students differ greatly in how satisfied they are with their lives, their motivation to achieve, how anxious they feel about their schoolwork, their expectations for the future, and their perceptions of being bullied at school or treated unfairly by their teachers both between and within countries. Students in some of the countries that top the PISA league tables in science and math report comparatively low satisfaction with life; but Finland, the Netherlands and Switzerland seem able to combine good learning outcomes and high satisfaction with life (Figure 2.5).

Figure 2.5 Academic learning and life satisfaction

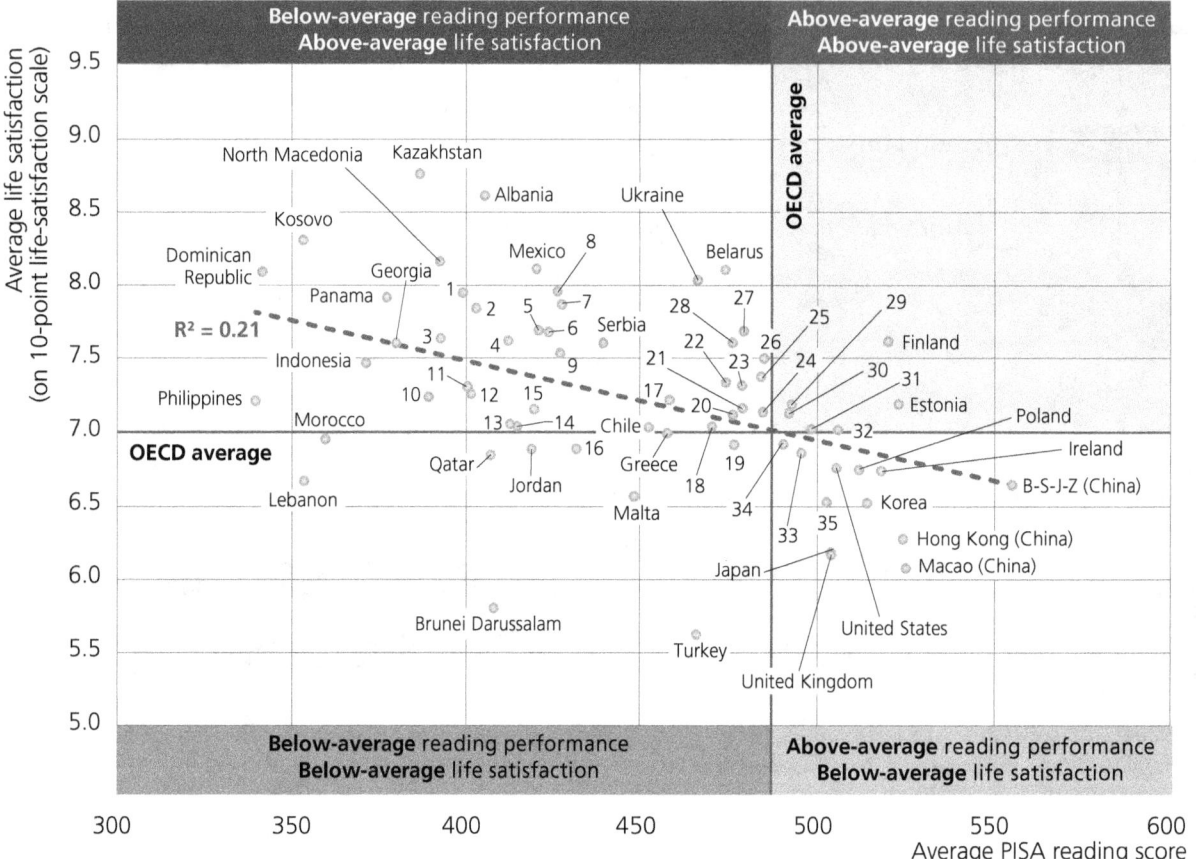

1. Saudi Arabia
2. Bosnia and Herzegovina
3. Colombia
4. Thailand
5. Montenegro
6. Moldova
7. Romania
8. Costa Rica
9. Uruguay
10. Baku (Azerbaijan)
11. Peru
12. Argentina
13. Brazil
14. Malaysia
15. Bulgaria
16. United Arab Emirates
17. Slovak Republic
18. Luxembourg
19. Italy
20. Hungary
21. Latvia
22. Iceland
23. Russia
24. Austria
25. Switzerland
26. Netherlands
27. Croatia
28. Lithuania
29. France
30. Portugal
31. Germany
32. Sweden
33. Slovenia
34. Czech Republic
35. Chinese Taipei

Source: (OECD, 2019[8]), *PISA 2018 Results (Volume III): What School Life Means for Students' Lives,* PISA, OECD Publishing, Paris, https://doi.org/10.1787/acd78851-en Tables III.B1.11.1 and I.B1.4, https://doi.org/10.1787/19963777.

It is tempting to equate low levels of life satisfaction in East Asia or elsewhere to long study hours but the data show no relationship between the time students spend studying, whether in or outside of school, and their satisfaction with life. And while educators often argue that anxiety is the natural consequence of testing overload, the frequency of tests is also unrelated to students' level of school-related anxiety.

There are other factors that make a difference to student well-being and much comes down to teachers, parents and schools.

For a start, PISA 2015 found that one major threat to students' feelings of belonging at school was their perceptions of negative relationships with their teachers. Students tended to report more positive relations with their teachers in "happy" schools (schools where students' life satisfaction is above the average in the country) reported much higher levels of support from their teacher than students in "unhappy" schools (Figure 2.6).

Figure 2.6 Teacher support in «happy» and «unhappy» schools (2015)

Index of teacher support in schools where students' life satisfaction is statistically significantly above/below the average in the country/economy

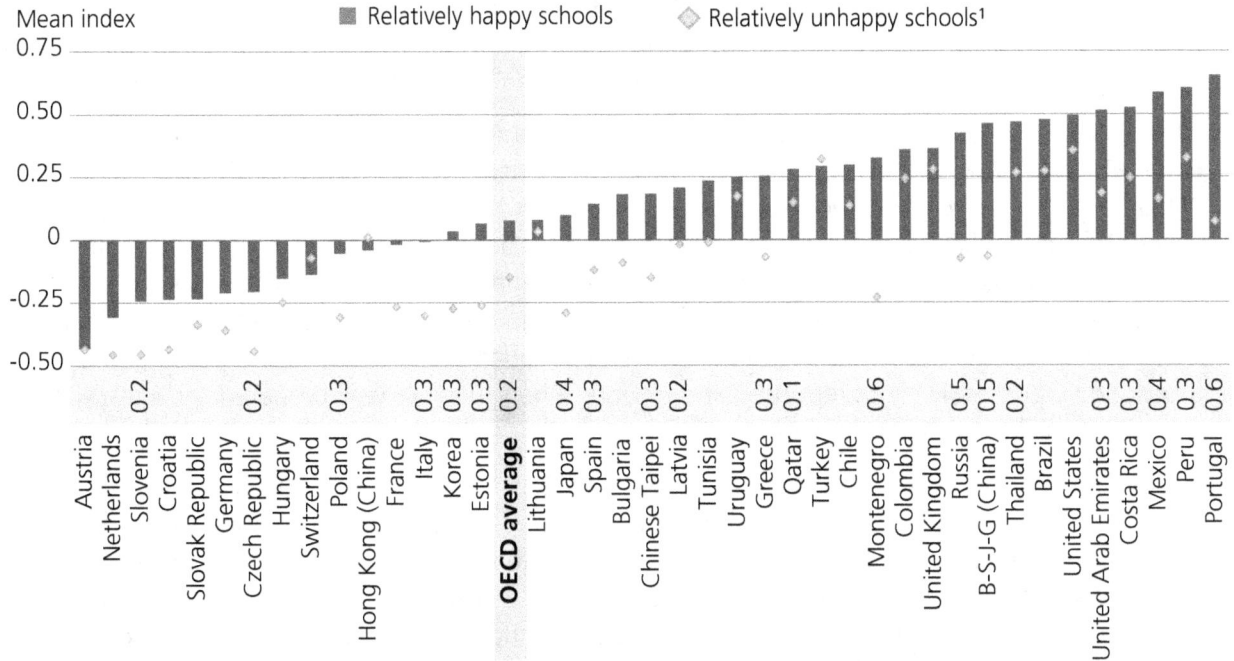

1. Relatively happy (unhappy) schools are schools where students' life satisfaction is statistically significantly above (below) the average in the country/economy.
Note: Statistically significant differences in the index of teacher support between schools that are relatively happy and those that are relatively unhappy are shown next to the country/economy name (see Annex A3).
Source: (OECD, 2017[7]), *PISA 2015 Results (Volume III): Students' Well-Being*, PISA, OECD Publishing, Paris, http://dx.doi.org/10.1787/9789264273856-en Table III.3.10. 2, http://dx.doi.org/10.1787/888933470657.

On average across countries, students who reported that their teacher is willing to provide help and is interested in their learning were also about 1.3 times more likely to feel that they belong at school. Conversely, students who reported some unfair treatment by their teachers were 1.7 times more likely to report feeling isolated at school. This is important. Teenagers look for strong social ties. They value acceptance, care and support from others. Adolescents who feel that they are part of a school community are more likely to perform better academically and be more motivated in school.

There are also big differences between countries on these measures. An average of three-quarters of students feel they belong at school, and in some of the highest performing education systems in terms of cognitive outcomes, including Chinese Taipei, Japan, the Netherlands, Vietnam, Finland, Korea, Estonia and Singapore, that share was even higher. But in France it was just 41%. In some countries, there were also large differences among students from different home backgrounds and in 23 countries and economies, students without an immigrant background reported a stronger sense of belonging than immigrant students, even after accounting for socio-economic status.

Of course, most teachers care about having positive relationships with their students but some teachers may be insufficiently prepared to deal with difficult students and classroom environments. Effective classroom management consists of far more than establishing and imposing rules, rewards and incentives to control behaviour. It involves practices and instructional techniques to create

Supporting the whole child

a learning environment that facilitates and supports active engagement in learning, encourages co-operation and promotes behaviour that benefits other people. A stronger focus on classroom and relationship management in professional development may give teachers better means to connect with their students and support their engagement at school. Teachers also need to collaborate and exchange information about students' difficulties, character and strengths with their colleagues so that they can collectively find the best approach to make students feel part of the school community.

While it is not the frequency of testing that affects student well-being, students' perception of tests as threatening has a clear influence on how anxious students feel about tests. On average across OECD countries, 59% of students reported in PISA 2015 that they often worry that taking a test will be difficult, and 66% reported that they worry about poor grades. Some 55% of students said they are very anxious about tests even if they are well prepared. Also here PISA suggests that there is much teachers can do about this: even after accounting for students' performance, gender and socio-economic status, students who said their teacher adapts the lesson to the class's needs and knowledge were less likely to report feeling anxious when they are well prepared for a test, or to report that they get very tense when they study.

Students were also less likely to report anxiety if their teacher provided individual help when they are struggling. By contrast, negative teacher-student relations seem to undermine students' confidence and lead to greater anxiety: On average across countries, students were about 62% more likely to get very tense when they study, and about 31% more likely to feel anxious before a test if they perceived that their teacher thought they are less smart than they thought they really are. Such anxiety may be students' reaction to, and interpretation of, the mistakes they make – or are afraid to make. Students may internalise mistakes as evidence that they are not smart enough. So teachers need to know how to help students develop a good understanding of their strengths and weaknesses, and an awareness of what they can do to overcome or mitigate their weaknesses. It is noteworthy that in all countries, girls reported greater schoolwork-related anxiety than boys and anxiety about schoolwork, homework and tests is negatively related to performance.

PISA 2018 results also show the negative association between students' perception of discrimination in their school and their level of respect for people from other cultures. On average across OECD countries, a rise of one unit in the index of perceived discrimination at school was associated with a decline of 0.18 of a unit in the index of respect for people from other cultures. This finding highlights the role of teachers in fighting discrimination by acting as role models, or perpetuating it by making discrimination routine.

Last but not least, parents can make a big difference too. Students whose parents reported "spending time just talking to my child", "eating the main meal with my child around a table" or "discussing how well my child is doing at school" daily or nearly every day were between 22% and 39% more likely to report high levels of life satisfaction. "Spending time just talking" is the parental activity most frequently and most strongly associated with students' life satisfaction. And it seems to matter for performance too: students whose parents reported "spending time just talking" were two-thirds of a school-year ahead in science learning, and even after accounting for social background, the advantage remains at one-third of a school year. The results are similar for eating meals with the children. The strength of this relationship is well beyond the impact of most school resources and school factors measured by PISA.

Students' perceptions of how interested their parents are in them and in their school life is also related to their own attitudes towards education and their motivation to study, and those relationships are particularly strong among low-performing students.

Parents can also help children manage test anxiety by encouraging them to trust in their ability to accomplish various academic tasks. PISA results show that, even after accounting for differences in performance and socio-economic status, girls who perceive that their parents encourage them to be confident in their abilities were 21% less likely to report that they feel tense when they study on average across OECD countries.

All in all, a clear way to promote students' well-being is to encourage all parents to be more involved with their children's interests and concerns, show interest in their school life, and be more aware of the challenges children face at school. The pandemic has opened up many opportunities for that, with many schools creating a new environment of co-operation with parents and communities. Teachers can be given better tools to enlist parents' support, and schools can address some critical deficiencies of disadvantaged children, such as the lack of a quiet space for studying. If parents and teachers establish relationships based on trust, schools can rely on parents as valuable partners in the cognitive and socio-emotional education of their students.

For many parents, spending time just talking to their child is a rare occurrence; others find it difficult to participate in their children's school life. These difficulties may be related to inflexible work schedules, lack of childcare services, or language barriers. But schools can do a lot to help parents overcome these barriers. They can first try to identify those parents who may be unable to participate in school activities. They can open flexible channels of communication such as scheduled phone or video calls, which are simple, but effective, solutions to accommodate busy parents who cannot easily leave work to attend school meetings. Governments can also take action by providing incentives to employers who adopt policies to improve the work-life balance.

While the influence of students' peers, teachers and parents can help foster students' sense of well-being, there are other factors at play. For instance, the nature and level of online activity shows interesting associations with their well-being. Students were asked how they feel about the time they spend on line and how they feel when they are engaged in online activities. Across OECD countries, most students agreed that "the Internet is a great resource for obtaining information" (88%) and that "it is very useful to have social networks on the Internet" (84%). Some 67% of students reported that they are excited to discover new digital devices and applications. The data also show that most students enjoy using various digital devices and the Internet, but many of them are at risk of excessive Internet use: On average 26% of students reported that they spend more than six hours per day on line during weekends, and 16% spend a similar amount of time on line during weekdays. And in most participating countries, extreme Internet use – more than six hours per day – has a negative relationship with students' life satisfaction. And with cyberbullying on the rise, the Internet can be as much a source of harassment as a tool for learning. There are no quick fixes for the risks of the digital era but schools can create opportunities for students to share their understanding of digital technology and challenges with adults and peers. They can also develop a clear incident-response plan for staff in the event of violations of safety norms and cyberbullying, provide access to in-school counselling to students involved in cyber-related incidents, and introduce a "digital safety" theme across school policies and practices.

Perhaps the most distressing threat to student well-being is bullying, and it can have serious consequences for the victim, the bully and the bystanders. Bullying can be inflicted directly through physical (hitting, punching or kicking) and verbal (name-calling or mocking) abuse. And then there is relational bullying, where some children are ignored, excluded from games or parties, rejected by peers, or are the victims of gossip and other forms of public humiliation and shaming. PISA highlights a significant prevalence of all these forms. On average across OECD countries, around

11% of students reported that they are frequently (at least a few times per month) made fun of, 7% reported that they are frequently left out of things, and 8% reported that they are frequently the object of nasty rumours in school. And around 4% of students – roughly one per class - reported that they are hit or pushed at least a few times per month, a percentage that varies from 1% to 9.5% across countries. Students who are frequently bullied may feel constantly insecure and on guard, and have clear difficulties finding their place at school. They tend to feel unaccepted and isolated and, as a result, are often withdrawn: on average across OECD countries, 42% of students who reported that they are frequently bullied – but only 15% of students who reported that they are not frequently bullied – reported feeling like an outsider at school.

There is no one-size-fits-all approach to preventing bullying. What emerges clearly from the PISA data, however, is that schools must do more to foster an environment of safety, tolerance and respect for children. A co-ordinated, international analysis of existing strategies and support mechanisms can shed light on what schools can do in the difficult struggle to assure students' safety at school, and what national and local authorities can do to support schools in this effort. Schools must work for more effective anti-bullying programmes, follow a whole-of-school approach that includes training for teachers on bullying behaviour and how to handle it and strategies to provide information to and engage with parents. Teachers need to communicate to students that they will not tolerate any form of bullying; and parents need to be involved in school planning and responses to bullying. In fact, victimisation by bullying is less frequently reported by students who said that their parents support them when they face difficulties at school. And yet, only 44% of the parents of frequently bullied students reported that they had exchanged ideas on parenting, family support, or the child's development with teachers over the previous academic year.

The challenges to students' well-being are numerous, and there are no simple solutions. But the findings from PISA show how teachers, schools and parents can make a real difference. Together, they can attend to students' psychological and social needs and help them develop a sense of control over their life and the resilience they need to be successful in life.

SUPPORTING TEACHERS SO THEY CAN SUPPORT STUDENTS

Schools are connected communities and efforts to improve the well-being of students should be accompanied by adequate support for teachers. Research has shown that teachers who report high levels of well-being tend to have better job performance and are better able to support school improvement.

Results from the Teaching and Learning International Survey (TALIS) 2018 show that, on average across OECD countries, 18% of lower secondary teachers reported experiencing a lot of stress in their work, albeit with a great deal of variation across countries. Among the top sources of stress reported by teachers ("quite a bit" or "a lot"), "having too much administrative work to do" (49%), "being held responsible for students' achievement" (44%) and "keeping up with changing requirements from local, municipal/regional, state or national/federal authorities" (41%) are prominent (Figure 2.7). The sources of stress reported by school leaders include "having too much administrative work to do" (69%), and "keeping up with changing requirements from local, municipal/regional, state or national/federal authorities" (55%).

Figure 2.7   Teachers' sources of stress

Percentage of lower secondary teachers for whom the following are sources of stress «quite a bit» or «a lot» (OECD average-31)

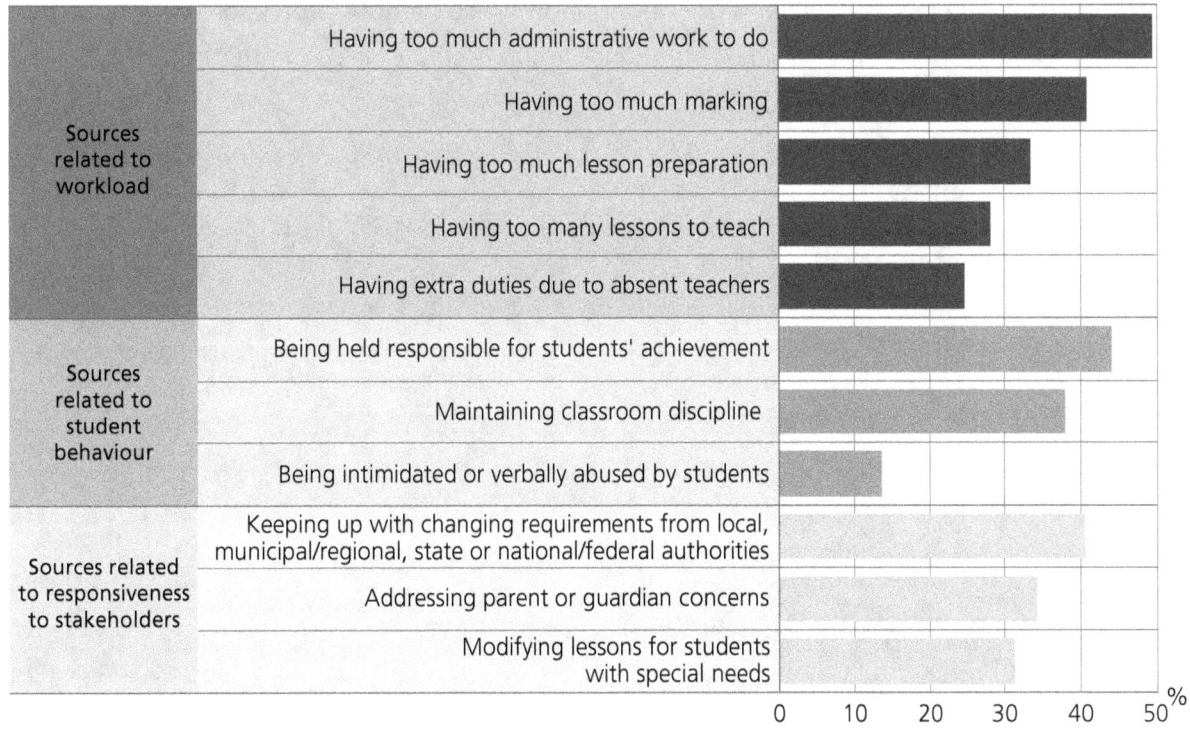

Note: Values are grouped by type of source and, within each group, ranked in descending order of the proportion of teachers reporting that the corresponding activities are a source of stress «quite a bit» or «a lot».
Source: (OECD, 2020[9]), *TALIS 2018 Results (Volume II): Teachers and School Leaders as Valued Professionals*, PISA, OECD Publishing, Paris, https://doi.org/10.1787/19cf08df-en Table II.2.43, http://dx.doi.org/10.1787/888934083392.

It is revealing to see that keeping up with changing requirements was a source of stress for around half of teachers and principals even prior to the pandemic, which has accelerated the pace of change. TALIS 2018 data also show that the estimated proportion of teachers reporting a lot of stress in their work increases more sharply with time spent on administrative tasks than with time spent on teaching (Figure 2.8). These results seem to suggest that teachers who spend many hours doing administrative tasks are more likely to report high levels of stress than those who spend many hours teaching in the classroom.

It is noteworthy that, according to TALIS, more experienced teachers are much more likely to report administrative sources of stress than their novice colleagues. It is not clear from the data whether this is because they have more administrative responsibilities within the school or because they are less likely than their younger colleagues to use digital tools to help them save time and gain efficiency in their administrative work.

Regression analyses shed light on patterns of attrition. They underline that teachers who reported experiencing a lot of stress in their work are more likely to report a wish to leave their work within the next five years in almost all countries and economies participating in TALIS. But the same analyses show that schools can moderate the relationship between stress and attrition. Indeed, teachers reporting satisfaction with their terms of employment apart from their salary (e.g. work schedule) are less likely to state they would leave teaching in the next five years (Figure 2.9). The analyses also show how teachers' tendency to report being satisfied with their terms of employment is related to staff participation in school governance and support for continuous professional development.

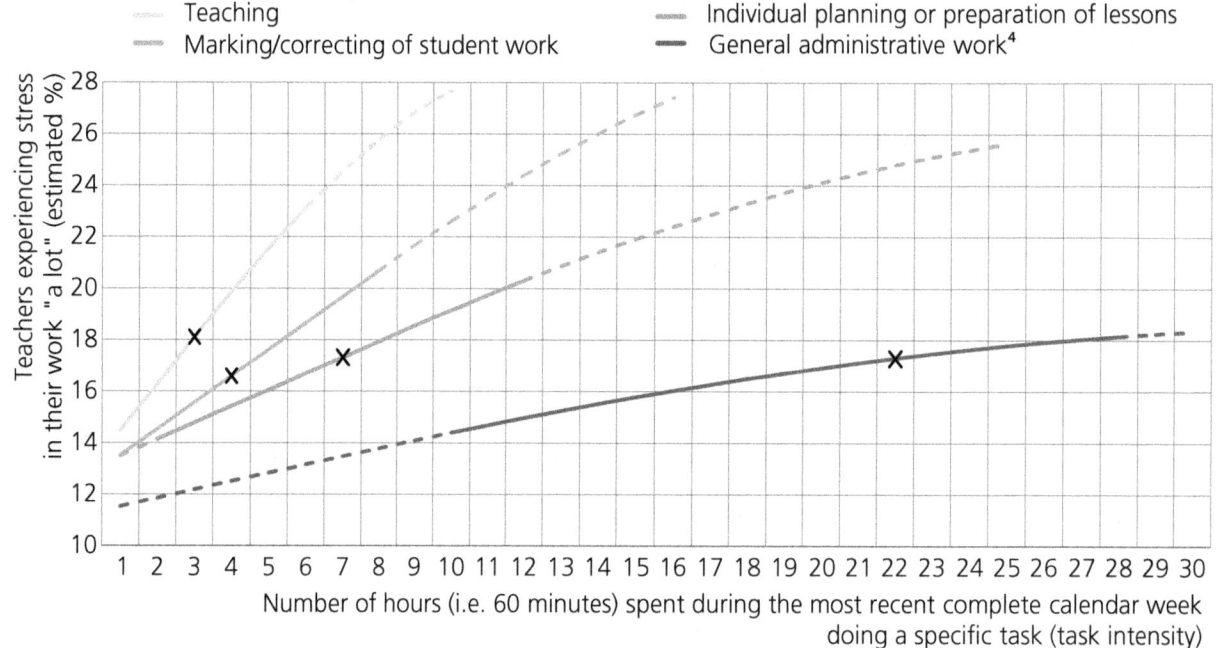

Figure 2.8 Relationship between teachers' experience of stress at work and task intensity

Estimated percentage of teachers experiencing stress in their work «a lot», by task intensity (OECD average-31) [1, 2, 3]

1. Results of binary logistic regression based on responses of lower secondary teachers.
2. The «X» in the figure represents the share of teachers experiencing stress in their work «a lot», given an average task intensity (OECD average-31).
3. Continuous lines cover 80% of the lower secondary teacher population across OECD countries and economies participating in TALIS; dashed lines are used to indicate the the expected percentage of teachers experiencing stress "a lot" in their work below and above the 1st and 9th decile of the task intensity distributions.
4. Estimates for "general administrative work" are obtained considering a task intensity ranging between 0 and 49 hours.
Source: (OECD, 2020[9]), *TALIS 2018 Results (Volume II): Teachers and School Leaders as Valued Professionals,* PISA, OECD Publishing, Paris, https://doi.org/10.1787/19cf08df-en, Figure II.2.10 http://dx.doi.org/10.1787/888934083411.

Figure 2.9 Intention to leave teaching within the next five years related to work-related stress and satisfaction with the terms of employment

Increased likelihood of desiring to change school and intention to leave teaching within the next five years related to work/related stress and satisfaction with the terms of employment[1,2,3,4]

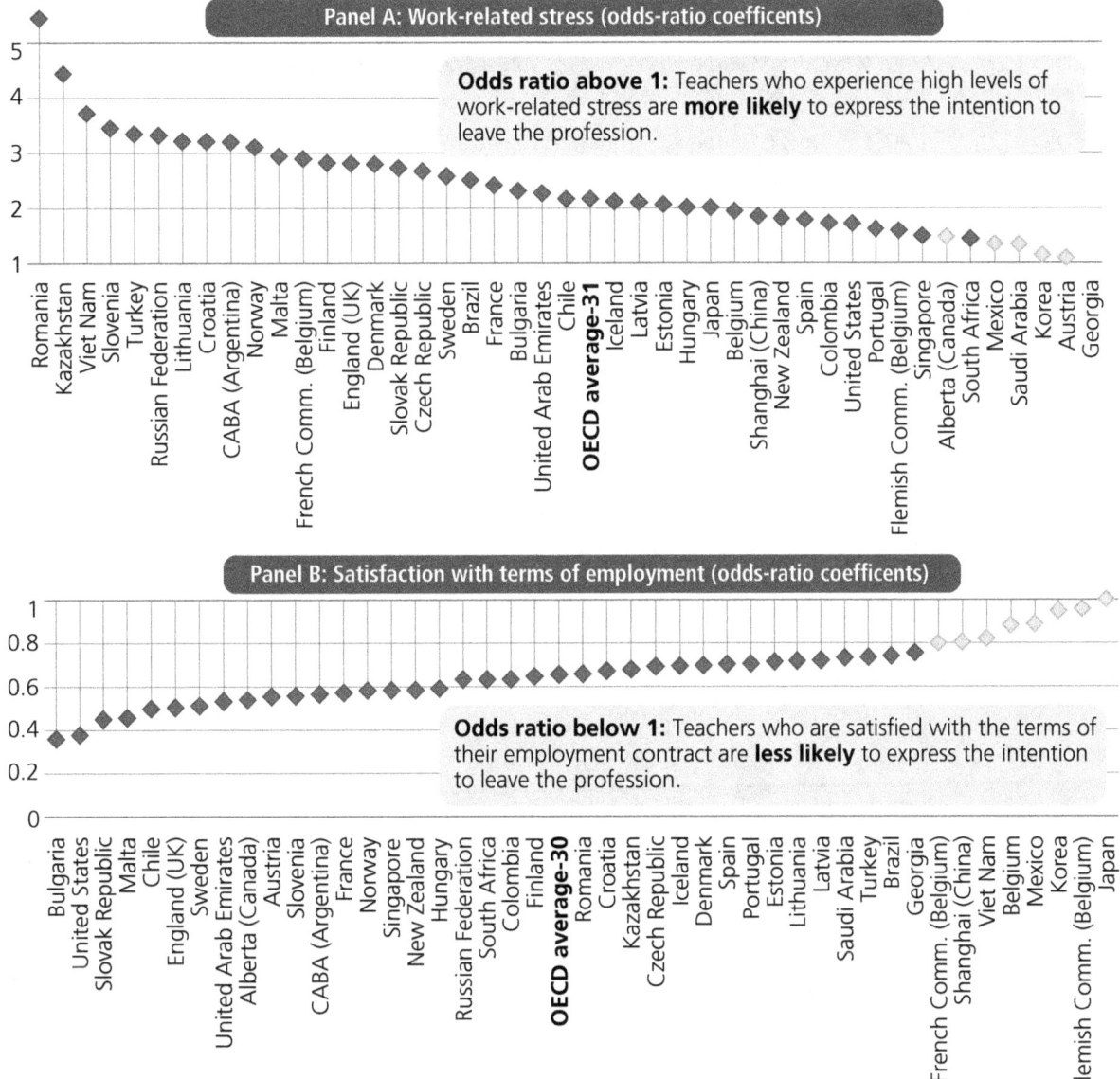

1. Results of binary logistic regressions based on responses of lower secondary teachers and principals.
2. An odds ratio indicates the degree to which an explanatory variable is associated with a categorical outcome variable. An odds ratio below one denotes a negative association; an odds ratio above one indicates a positive association; and an odds ratio of one means that there is no association.
3. The predictor is a dummy variable: the reference category refers to not being satisfied with other terms of the teaching contract/employment («Disagree» or «Strongly disagree»).
4. Controlling for the following: teacher characteristics (gender, age, years of experience as a teacher at current school, working full-time); classroom composition (students from socio-economically disadvantaged homes); and school characteristics (school location index, school type and school size).

Note: Statistically significant coefficients are marked in a darker tone. Countries and economies are ranked in descending order of the likelihood of desiring to change school related to satisfaction with the terms of the employment contract.

Source: (OECD, 2020[9]), TALIS 2018 Results (Volume II): Teachers and School Leaders as Valued Professionals, TALIS, OECD Publishing, Paris https://doi.org/10.1787/19cf08df-en, Tables II.2.67 http://dx.doi.org/10.1787/888934084285 and II.3.76 http://dx.doi.org/10.1787/888934084304.

REFERENCES

OECD (2020), *PISA 2018 Results (Volume VI): Are Students Ready to Thrive in an Interconnected World?*, OECD Publishing, Paris, https://doi.org/10.1787/d5f68679-en. [6]

OECD (2020), *TALIS 2018 Results (Volume II): Teachers and School Leaders as Valued Professionals*, OECD Publishing, Paris, https://doi.org/10.1787/19cf08df-en. [9]

OECD (2019), *PISA 2018 Results (Volume III): What School Life Means for Students' Lives,* OECD Publishing, Paris, https://doi.org/10.1787/acd78851-en. [8]

OECD (2017), *PISA 2015 Results (Volume III): Students' Well-Being*, OECD Publishing, Paris, https://doi.org/10.1787/19963777. [7]

03
REDEFINING EQUITY IN THE 21ST CENTURY

How can governments and teacher organisations collaborate on strategies that are relentlessly focused on equity to advance the future of education and to ensure an excellent education for all?

What wise parents want for their children is what the government should facilitate for all children. Children from wealthier families will find many open doors to a successful life. But children from poor families often have just one chance in life, and that is a good school that offers them an opportunity to develop their potential. Those who miss that boat rarely catch up as subsequent education opportunities in life tend to reinforce early education outcomes.

Achieving greater equity in education is not just a social-justice imperative, it is also a way to use resources more efficiently, and to increase the supply of knowledge and skills that fuel economic growth and promote social cohesion. Economies are rapidly shifting towards regional hubs of production, linked together by global chains of information and goods, but concentrated where comparative advantage can be built and renewed. This makes the distribution of knowledge and wealth so crucial, and that is intimately tied to the distribution of educational opportunities.

Instead of dealing with the consequences of social and economic inequality through the redistribution of wealth, education provides a unique lever to address the sources of inequality and foster social mobility. One of the most distressing outcomes of the pandemic has been how it has reinforced the many inequities in education systems at individual, institutional and systemic levels.

While many efforts are underway to address the immediate consequences, the pandemic also offers an opportunity to refocus on inclusion and address the more structural and fundamental inequalities inherent in education systems. The 21st-century challenge of educational equity is not just to provide all learners with the same learning opportunities but to cherish and address the differences of learners. OECD's Strengths Through Diversity project offers a framework for this, the main elements of which are outlined in the following.

INCLUSIVE TEACHING: DESIGN ELEMENTS TO PROMOTE MORE EQUITABLE AND INCLUSIVE EDUCATION

Inclusive access to education opportunities is an obvious prerequisite to promote more equitable and inclusive education, and this an area where most countries have made some progress in recent decades. The challenge is now to shift emphasis from inclusive access to success. To achieve this, three main elements are key: inclusive pedagogy, curriculum and assessment. These elements can be promoted by individual teachers, teacher organisations and/or education systems. Effective collaboration among governments and teacher organisations can support implementation in everyday teaching practices. Table 3.1 provides an overview of each element as well as practical examples of strategies promoted by organisations and governments across OECD countries.

Table 3.2 summarises evidence from OECD countries on effective interventions aimed at promoting inclusive pedagogy, curriculum and assessment among prospective and in-service teachers. Several examples concern strategies carried out by diverse stakeholders, including teacher organisations and governments.

Table 3.1 [1/2] Three main elements for inclusive teaching

Element	Conceptualisation	Rationale	Practical examples
Inclusive pedagogy	A pedagogy can be defined as "repeated patterns or sets of teaching and learning practices that shape the interaction between teachers and learners" (Peterson et al., 2018, p. 8[2]). An inclusive pedagogical approach is "underpinned by a shift in pedagogical thinking from an approach that works for most learners existing alongside something 'additional' or 'different' for those (some) who experience difficulties" (Florian and Black-Hawkins, 2011[3]).	The inclusive pedagogical approach aims to provide an answer to questions concerning how individual students can receive the support they need without being treated differently from other students in the classroom. Key elements of inclusive pedagogical approaches are supporting sense of belonging, self-efficacy and engagement of all students (Florian and Sprat, 2013[4]) (Alfassi, 2003[5]; Florian and Sprat, 2013[4]; Sanger, 2020[6]). Inclusive pedagogies should be informed by the diverse experiences of the students in the classroom through active dialogue with them (Dewsbury and Brame, 2019[7]).	Designing and assessing inclusive pedagogical approaches: • E.g. Youcubed, a Stanford-based platform providing pedagogical approaches for engaging all students in mathematics (Youcubed - Stanford Graduate School of Education, 2020[8]). • E.g. the Inclusive Pedagogical Approach in Action (IPAA) is a framework designed to support teachers in developing and evaluating inclusive pedagogical practices to inclusively address the needs of all students (Florian and Sprat, 2013[4]).
Inclusive curriculum	An inclusive curriculum "takes into consideration and caters for the diverse needs, previous experiences, interests and personal characteristics of all learners. It attempts to ensure that all students are part of the shared learning experiences of the classroom and that equal opportunities are provided regardless of learner differences" (UNESCO, 2020[9]).	Curricula must be designed, presented and taught to include a multiplicity of perspectives and voices. • Diversity and inclusion can be promoted in the selection of the content being taught or through more indirect tools; • To design inclusive curricula, teachers must recognise their own cultural frames of reference and understand how their assumptions and beliefs influence their teaching; • Teachers should avoid tokenising students.	Designing a diverse and inclusive curriculum: • In Early Childhood Education and Care (ECEC): more diverse and inclusive representation of social identities through dolls and toys (O'neill, McDonald and Jones, 2018[10]; Perlman, Kankesan and Zhang, 2010[11]; Straske, 2019[12]); refraining from adopting and teaching gender-colour coding; providing a rainbow of skin colours beyond the traditional peach colour (Wong and Hines, 2015[13]). • In Physical Education: providing appropriate content and types of activities and adequate forms of deliveries (OECD, 2019[14]). Assessing diversity and inclusion in the curriculum: • The Culturally Responsive Curriculum Scorecard is a tool designed by the Metropolitan Center for Research on Equity and the Transformation of Schools to support teachers and other education stakeholders to assess diversity, inclusion and cultural responsiveness (Bryan-Gooden, Hester and & Peoples, 2019[15]).

Source: Adapted from (Brussino, Forthcoming[27]), "Building capacity for inclusive teaching: Policies and practices to prepare teachers for diversity and inclusion", *OECD Education Working Papers*, OECD Publishing, Paris.

Table 3.1 [2/2] Three main elements for inclusive teaching

Element	Conceptualisation	Rationale	Practical examples
Inclusive assessment	Formative and summative assessment should be designed and implemented taking into account the diverse needs and learning styles of all students.	Teachers who actively adopt formative assessments appear to be better prepared to meet diverse student needs (OECD, 2008[16]). It can support teachers in adjusting their teaching methods to meet the diversity of student needs.	Teachers can develop and implement inclusive assessment by: • Scaffolding summative assessments into smaller assignments throughout the unit (Kenyon, 2018[17]); • Acknowledging class participation as an assessment component (Kenyon, 2018[17]); • Proposing students a diversity of assessment typologies (Kenyon, 2018[17]); • Providing timely and frequent feedback (Columbia Center for Teaching and Learning, 2020[18]); • Employing blind-grading techniques, group and peer evaluations, and student self-evaluations.

Source: Adapted from (Brussino, Forthcoming[27]), "Building capacity for inclusive teaching: Policies and practices to prepare teachers for diversity and inclusion", *OECD Education Working Papers*, OECD Publishing, Paris.

Table 3.2 [1/2] Three main elements for inclusive teaching

Element	Examples of interventions	Impact
Inclusive pedagogy	• Initial teacher education	• Evidence shows positive outcomes of developing pre-service training on culturally responsive teaching, through critically reflective pedagogies aimed at engaging prospective teachers in critical reflection and awareness of their own beliefs and assumptions (Burbank, Ramirez and Bates, 2016[19]).
	• Formal professional learning and training	• Evidence from pedagogical training for 200 teachers at the University of Helsinki, Finland, shows that promoting professional learning programmes aimed at enhancing teachers' pedagogical skills has considerable positive effects on how teachers develop self-efficacy and student-centred teaching approaches (Postareff, Lindblom-Ylänne and Nevgi, 2007[20]). • By promoting inclusive pedagogical approaches through in-service training, there can be positive effects on the way in which teachers develop beliefs, attitudes, self-efficacy and inclusive teaching strategies (Brennan, King and Travers, 2019[21]).

Source: Adapted from (Brussino, Forthcoming[27]), "Building capacity for inclusive teaching: Policies and practices to prepare teachers for diversity and inclusion", *OECD Education Working Papers*, OECD Publishing, Paris.

Table 3.2 [2/2] Three main elements for inclusive teaching

	Examples of interventions	Impact
Inclusive pedagogy	• Horizontal professional learning opportunities	• Evidence from evaluation of horizontal professional learning programme "On the Shoulders of Giants" in Spain shows that teachers participating in the training successfully engage in dialogic teacher education. The training not only positively affects the practices and attitudes teachers develop in the classroom; it also encourages horizontal co-operation and knowledge sharing among teachers. Key impacts include transforming teaching practices of individual teachers and increasingly informing teaching practices through evidence-based research (Rodriguez et al., 2020[22]).
Inclusive curriculum	• Promoting diversity and inclusion in the curriculum through open dialogue • Integrating content in the curriculum	• Courses encouraging open dialogue among students on ethnicity-related matters positively influence student attitudes towards others (Zirkel, 2008[23]). • Similar results are shown regarding courses integrating content on sexual orientation. Even when curricula marginally incorporate cultural and ethnic diversity-related content, this nonetheless leads to better academic outcomes, self-confidence and engagement for students across education levels
Inclusive assessment	• Promoting a positive understanding of critical feedback • Providing frequent and timely feedback	• Encouraging students, particularly those from minority backgrounds, to view critical feedback as a sign of teachers' high standards, while also promoting a belief that students are potentially able to meet those standards, leads to eliminatinZg students' perception of bias or unfairness in the feedback received (Cohen, Steele and Ross, 1999[25]). • Critical feedack has significant impact on the learning outcomes of Black students in urban settings across the United States, also leading to a decrease in achievement gaps between Black and white students (Yeager, Walton and Cohen, 2013[26]). • Receiving frequent feedback correlates to higher self-reported life satisfaction and can also contribute to enhancing emotional resilience among students from migration backgrounds (OECD, 2018[27]).

Source: Adapted from (Brussino, Forthcoming[27]), "Building capacity for inclusive teaching: Policies and practices to prepare teachers for diversity and inclusion", *OECD Education Working Papers*, OECD Publishing, Paris.

PROMOTING EQUITABLE AND INCLUSIVE TEACHING STRATEGIES IN THE VIRTUAL CLASSROOM

In online learning, effective interactions among students and between students and teachers are crucial to supporting teaching and learning for the diversity of teachers and students involved. In turn, the ways in which teachers manage interactions in the virtual classroom affect student learning.

Managing online interactions is key to developing students' sense of belonging and enhancing motivation and participation for the diversity of students in the virtual classroom.

In online platforms teachers have a number of arrangements at their disposal to promote inclusive teaching. Yale University's Poorvu Center for Teaching and Learning provides guidelines for instructors to promote inclusive teaching via online platforms, through a variety of options, such as gallery view, break-out rooms, display names and cameras (Table 3.3).

Table 3.3 Inclusive teaching through online platforms

Arrangement	Rationale
Gallery view	It is suitable when teachers want to promote synchronous dialogue among students in the virtual classroom.
Break-out rooms	It provides teachers opportunities to divide students into smaller groups to engage in discussions or carry out tasks. The assignment of students to different rooms can be carried out either randomly, manually or through self-selection.
Display names	Students can modify the name displayed in the virtual classroom to enhance safe and enabling environments for all students. For example, this can promote the inclusion of gender-diverse students. In their name, teachers can display their personal pronouns and ask students to do so too.
Cameras	Teachers should be aware that keeping cameras on for a prolonged time can lead to students and/or teachers experiencing fatigue. Additionally, due to a diversity of issues such as geographic location and socio-economic status, students may have poor access to high-quality ICT devices and Internet. Teachers should keep this in mind as well as other factors (e.g. the personal space where students connect from) that may be leading students to keep their cameras off in the virtual classroom.

Source: (Yale, n.d.[36]), Classroom Seating Arrangements (Accessed on 15 September, 2021).

ENHANCING SCHOOL-LEVEL COLLABORATION TO PROMOTE MORE EQUITABLE AND INCLUSIVE EDUCATION FOR ALL

School-level collaboration is key to promoting teacher capacity to inclusively teach to all students and support teachers' work in the classroom. Partnerships for inclusive teaching do not only include promoting horizontal professional learning opportunities, such as professional learning communities, but also enhancing active collaboration among school staff at different levels, including school leaders and administrators.

In particular, an inclusive school leadership and management is key to set collaborative school environments that adequately support inclusive teaching practices. An inclusive school leadership aims to promote participation and inclusion of all stakeholders, value diversity and ensure that all students receive a high-quality education. It has three main leadership dimensions:

- Transformative: enhancing agency, facilitating innovation, change and learning;
- Distributed: establishing a collective and shared leadership with a scope within and outside the school
- Instructional: setting a vision concerning the academic and broader well-being of all students.

Table 3.4 summarises some of the available strategies, policies and practices across OECD countries to promote school-level collaboration for equity and inclusion.

Table 3.4 Strategies to guide teachers through inclusive school leadership and management

Strategy	Rationale	Policies and practices
Inclusive school leadership	School leaders play an important role in fostering an inclusive school environment by promoting collaboration and professional learning among school staff (McLeskey, Billingsley and Waldron, 2016[28]). An inclusive school leadership also drives the framing of new meanings of diversity and inclusion, promotes an inclusive school culture and inclusive instructional programmes, as well as consolidates partnerships between schools and communities (Riehl, 2000[29]).	In New Brunswick, Canada, Policy 322 on Inclusive Education of 2013 establishes the requirements for inclusive public schools and school districts in the province. • It sets out key requirements for an inclusive school leadership, e.g. promoting adequate professional learning opportunities for teachers and school staff and supporting teachers and school staff in the implementation of inclusive practices. • Principals should also check that all academic and behavioural interventions implemented within the school are evidence-based and aimed at supporting diverse student needs and learning styles. • They are also required to ensure that school- and community-level partnerships aim to achieve individual student growth goals identified in personalised learning plans (New Brunswick Department of Education and Early Childhood Development, 2013[30]).
Partnerships at different levels	School-level collaboration is key to promote teachers' capacity to inclusively teach to all students and support their work in the classroom (UNESCO, 2020[31]). Partnerships for inclusive teaching do not only include promoting horizontal professional learning opportunities, such as professional learning communities but also enhancing active collaboration among school staff at different levels, including school leaders and administrators.	In Sweden, the Collaboration for the Best School ("Samverkan för bästa skola", SBS) is a programme aimed at supporting schools with low student outcomes and graduation rates that have witnessed challenges in improving student achievement alone. It aims to: • Enhance partnerships among different stakeholders at different levels, including higher education institutions and school leaders. • Connect key agents for school improvement, in particular principals, vice-principals and first teachers, with available research to drive school improvement. • Reduce gaps within school management and promote more equitable school environments for all students through support provided to school leaders and school management boards (Glaés-Coutts and Nilsson, 2021[32]).
Inclusive school management	An inclusive school leadership and management is key to set collaborative school environments that adequately support inclusive teaching practices.	New Zealand provides comprehensive guidelines for school management boards to drive school-level change towards more inclusive learning environments for all students, with a focus on students with special education needs. • Key areas for action include setting a vision and a direction; understanding current school performance; planning for student success; supporting teachers; aligning school budget to priorities; and monitoring performance. • For each priority area, the guidelines provide key questions for the school board to guide and monitor their work to promote diversity and inclusion within the institution of reference (New Zealand Ministry of Education, 2013[33]).

Source: Adapted from (Brussino, Forthcoming[27]), "Building capacity for inclusive teaching: Policies and practices to prepare teachers for diversity and inclusion", *OECD Education Working Papers*, OECD Publishing, Paris.

ALLOCATING HIGH-QUALITY TEACHERS TO DISADVANTAGED SCHOOLS TO PROMOTE MORE EQUITABLE AND INCLUSIVE EDUCATION FOR ALL

Schools in more disadvantaged settings face greater challenges in promoting student well-being and learning. They often lack high-performing internal capacity to address student needs and support their learning. This can be further hindered by weaker family and community networks of support. Matching high-quality teachers to disadvantaged school settings is key to promoting equitable and inclusive learning environments for all students. Good, supportive school leaders and managers in disadvantaged settings is all the more crucial as novice teachers are more likely to be overemployed in disadvantaged schools compared to more experienced teachers. In these schools it is important to effectively match human resources with needs. Across countries, diverse mechanisms are in place to match high-performing teachers with schools with the highest needs for high-quality professionals (see Table 3.5).

Table 3.5 [1/2] Strategies to match high-quality teachers to disadvantaged schools

Strategy	Rationale	Policies and practices
Assigning more experienced teachers to disadvantaged settings, novice teachers to less disadvantaged ones	Across countries, novice teachers are overemployed in more disadvantaged school environments while also being less equipped to meet the challenges there (see Chapter 3). Assigning novice teachers to less disadvantaged environments aims to smooth their transition and mitigate high attrition (OECD, 2019[34]). This can be achieved through diverse financial and non-financial approaches.	Centralised/decentralised systems (OECD, 2018[35]): • Countries with centralised mechanisms of teacher allocation and compensation can create a fixed-term assignment for novice teachers that specifically assigns them to less challenging settings. • In more decentralised systems, increasing school budgets and autonomy cam help attract and retain high-performing teachers. Salary incentives: • In Spain, a regional credit system allows teachers in disadvantaged and diverse school settings to obtain extra credits to use for career development (OECD, 2017[36]). • Turkey implements a similar framework (OECD, 2017[36]). • To be effective, these salary incentives may need to be significant (OECD, 2019[37]).
Incentives and rotation schemes	Incentives and rotation schemes can support the transfer of high-quality teachers to schools with less effective teachers and promote access to high-quality teaching for all students.	• In Japan, there are mandatory rotation mechanisms requiring teachers to relocate to different schools periodically. Rules for such mechanisms are decided by local education authorities (Schleicher, 2020[38]). • In Korea, teachers are expected to change school every five years. To attract teachers into more disadvantaged school settings, there is a set of financial and non-financial incentives, e.g. higher salaries, smaller classrooms, awarding credits and promotions, and allowing teachers to choose the next school to work (OECD, 2018[35]).

Source: Adapted from (Brussino, Forthcoming[27]), "Building capacity for inclusive teaching: Policies and practices to prepare teachers for diversity and inclusion", *OECD Education Working Papers*, OECD Publishing, Paris.

Table 3.5 [2/2] Strategies to match high-quality teachers to disadvantaged schools

Strategy	Rationale	Policies and practices
Identifying and preparing high-quality prospective teachers for disadvantaged school settings	In initial teacher education high-performing prospective teachers are identified and trained specifically to teach in disadvantaged and diverse settings.	• In Australia, the High Achieving Teachers programme provides alternative employment-based pathways into teaching for high-achieving individuals committed to pursuing a teaching career. Participants are placed in teaching positions in Australian secondary schools with shortages of teachers. Students at disadvantaged schools will benefit when high-achieving university graduates, including those with a science, technology, engineering and mathematics (STEM) degree and those from a regional background, are recruited to teach at their school (Australian Government Department of Education, Skills and Employment, 2021[39]).

Source: Adapted from (Brussino, Forthcoming[27]), "Building capacity for inclusive teaching: Policies and practices to prepare teachers for diversity and inclusion", *OECD Education Working Papers*, OECD Publishing, Paris.

PROMOTING TEACHER DIVERSITY TO SUPPORT THE LEARNING AND WELL-BEING OUTCOMES OF DIVERSE STUDENTS

Table 3.6 provides an overview of the impact of having a more diverse and inclusive teaching workforce, both on diverse students as well as on the overall classroom. Available evidence mainly refers to teacher-student congruence based on ethnicity coming from the United States.

Table 3.6 [1/2] The impacts of teacher-student congruence

Some of the effects of teacher-student congruence in terms of shared belonging to ethnic groups and national minorities on diverse students and the overall classroom

	Policies and practices
Academic outcomes	• Evidence from the United States shows a small but significant positive impact of teacher-student ethnic congruence on reading and maths performances (Dee, 2004[40]), Clotfelter, Ladd, and Vigdor (Clotfelter, Ladd and Vigdor, 2007[41]; Dee, 2004[40]; Egalite, Kisida and Winters, 2015[42]). These effects seem to be particularly true for lower-performing students (Egalite, Kisida and Winters, 2015[42]). • A comprehensive review of studies carried out between 1998 and 2015 finds that teacher-student ethnic congruence led to 0.02-0.06 SD in student reading performance and 0.03 to 0.11 in maths performance, with larger effects for Black teacher.
Teacher perceptions on student participation, performance and ability	• There appear to be higher academic outcomes and teacher perceptions for students sharing similar identities to teachers, including ethnicity and gender (Dee, 2005[44]; Gershenson, Holt and Papageorge, 2016[45]; Grissom and Redding, 2016[46]).

Source: Adapted from (Brussino, Forthcoming[27]), "Building capacity for inclusive teaching: Policies and practices to prepare teachers for diversity and inclusion", *OECD Education Working Papers*, OECD Publishing, Paris.

Table 3.6 [2/2] **The impacts of teacher-student congruence**
Some of the effects of teacher-student congruence in terms of shared belonging to ethnic groups and national minorities on diverse students and the overall classroom

	Policies and practices
Student engagement, participation and future aspirations	• Teacher-student congruence in terms of shared belonging to marginalised groups may also have positive effects on reducing student absences, suspensions and early dropouts. • Ouazad (2014[47]) finds that teachers' evaluations of disruptive behaviours improve significantly with Black teacher-student congruence, with a decrease by 28-38% in suspensions rates among Black students. • Holt and Gershenson (2019[48]) find a causal relationship between having teachers sharing students' ethnic backgrounds and lower student absences and suspensions. • A large-scale analysis of administrative data and disciplinary records across public schools in North Carolina, United States, investigate the effects of Black teachers on Black students' exclusionary discipline (e.g. in-school suspensions, out-of-school suspensions and expulsions). It finds that teacher-student congruence is associated with decreased exclusionary discipline across education levels from elementary to secondary schools, irrespective of gender and socio-economic status (Lindsay and Hart, 2017[49]). • Assigning a Black male student to a Black teacher between grades 3 and 5 seems to have a significant effect on reducing the likelihood that the student drops out of school. This holds especially true for students from lower socio-economic backgrounds. When exposed to at least one Black teacher between grades 3 and 5, Black students from lower socio-economic backgrounds – irrespective of gender – are more likely to have stronger aspirations to attend higher education (Gershenson et al., 2017[50]).
Outcomes in the rest of the classroom	• A study on the impact of teachers from immigrant backgrounds on student performance in secondary schools across the United States shows that teachers from immigrant backgrounds have no negative effect on non-immigrant students' academic achievements. It also assesses that white immigrant teachers appear to be more effective teachers than native teachers (Seah, 2018[51]).

Source: Adapted from (Brussino, Forthcoming[27]), "Building capacity for inclusive teaching: Policies and practices to prepare teachers for diversity and inclusion", *OECD Education Working Papers*, OECD Publishing, Paris.

WORKING TOWARDS EQUITY IN THE DISTRIBUTION OF STAFF ACROSS SCHOOLS

Finally, an equitable distribution of educational resources to schools is of fundamental importance. Through formula-based funding approaches that account for the nature of the student body many countries have made progress in aligning material resources with needs. However, the challenge is to align human resources with needs. OECD's Review of the Effectiveness of Resource Allocation in Schools offers a number of lessons for promoting an equitable distribution of staff across the education system. These are outlined in the following:

Ensuring equitable and transparent resource allocations for school staffing

A key to equitable distribution of staff across schools lies in the design and implementation of equitable funding allocation mechanisms. To support greater equity within a school system, funding systems should be based on a balance between targeted and regular funding. For the distribution of regular funding for current expenditures such as staff salaries, the use of a well-designed funding formula can provide an efficient, equitable and transparent method of distributing resources, and a clear framework for debates on the sufficiency and equity of resource allocations.

Where responsibilities for the funding of staff are decentralised, sub-national authorities need to have adequate revenues to meet the needs of their schools and students, and relevant capacity to fulfil their funding responsibilities. Both can be supported through well-designed equalisation mechanisms. Many countries show a considerable financial commitment to supporting students at risk of under-performance. This includes additional resources that can be used for school staffing. This focus on additional inputs needs to be matched with sufficient attention to monitoring the outcomes for different student groups. Thematic studies on the use of resources for equity are one option for monitoring the equity of the school system.

No matter how well designed a funding allocation mechanism is, however, there will always be winners and losers when implementing a new model unless additional resources are made available. Experiences in many countries therefore highlight the importance of effectively managing the political economy of funding reform and of having a realistic estimate of the costs involved.

Reviewing regulations and criteria for recruitment, allocation and transfers

In a number of school systems, teachers' interests rather than students' needs drive the distribution of teachers. Rules and regulations for the selection and transfer of teachers such as weight of seniority together with teachers' preferences for working in particular contexts may channel the best teachers to the most advantaged schools. Beginning teachers are then mostly assigned to schools that are more difficult, potentially harming student learning and teacher retention and satisfaction. Regulations that give priority to candidates with specific types of appointment or levels of experience may also make it more difficult to match the mix of experiences and skills of teaching staff to school contexts. To address these concerns, it could prove useful to review such regulations, creating greater flexibility for appointments regardless of employment status or experience. Recognising experience in difficult or remote schools for teachers' career progression is a further possibility.

Providing incentives for teachers and school leaders to work in high-need areas

In some contexts, monetary incentives have shown promising results in distributing teachers where they are most needed. One consideration then is to put in place financial incentives for staff to work in areas of need. These include higher salaries in schools enrolling high proportions of students from disadvantaged backgrounds; differential pay for particular expertise; or scholarships and subsidies for working in disadvantaged schools. But such policies will work differently depending on the design and size of the incentives and the general framework for employment and career progression. Financial incentive schemes therefore require adequate evaluation and monitoring. This will also inform the dialogue between decision makers and stakeholders and facilitate implementation and potential adjustments. In some contexts, financial incentives have been shown to be effective in attracting teachers to rural schools, but less so for remote schools, for example.

Of course, non-financial incentives also matter, although more needs to be understood about the relative importance of financial and non-financial aspects. Research shows that most teachers are highly motivated by the intrinsic benefits of teaching, namely working with children and young people and helping them develop and learn. Professional factors such as opportunities to take on extra responsibilities and strong leadership and collegiality in professional learning also need to be considered. So do working conditions such as preparation time, accountability demands, class size or facilities. In other words, it is essential to ensure that all schools, and especially those in challenging circumstances, provide attractive conditions for staff to work in.

REFERENCES

Alfassi, M. (2003), "Promoting the will and skill of students at academic risk: An evaluation of an instructional design geared to foster achievement, self-efficacy and motivation", *Journal of Instructional Psychology,* Vol. 30/1, pp. 28-40. [13]

Australian Government Department of Education, Skills and Employment (2021), *Teaching and School Leadership - Alternative Pathways,* https://www.dese.gov.au/teaching-and-school-leadership/alternative-pathways#:~:text=High%20Achieving%20Teachers%20Program,-The%20Australian%20Government&text=Each%20pathway%20proactively%20recruits%20-and,schools%20experiencing%20teacher%20workforce%20shor (accessed on 13 April 2021). [49]

Brennan, A., F. King and J. Travers (2019), "Supporting the enactment of inclusive pedagogy in a primary school", *International Journal of Inclusive Education,* pp. 1-18, https://doi.org/10.1080/13603116.2019.1625452. [30]

Brussino, O. (Forthcoming), *Building capacity for inclusive teaching: Policies and practices to prepare teachers for diversity and inclusion,* OECD Publishing. [27]

Bryan-Gooden, J., M. Hester and L. & Peoples (2019), *Culturally Responsive Curriculum Scorecard,* New York University, https://steinhardt.nyu.edu/sites/default/files/2020-12/CRE%20Scorecard%20Revised%20Aug%202020.pdf (accessed on 26 January 2021). [23]

Burbank, M., L. Ramirez and A. Bates (2016), "The Impact of Critically Reflective Teaching: A Continuum of Rhetoric", *Action in Teacher Education*, Vol. 38/2, pp. 104-119, https://doi.org/10.1080/01626620.2016.1155095. [28]

Clotfelter, C., H. Ladd and J. Vigdor (2007), "How and Why Do Teacher Credentials Matter for Student Achievement", *NBER Working Papers*, No. 12828, National Bureau of Economic Research, http://dx.doi.org/10.3386/w12828. [51]

Cohen, G., C. Steele and L. Ross (1999), "The Mentor's Dilemma: Providing Critical Feedback Across the Racial Divide", *Personality and Social Psychology Bulletin,* Vol. 25/10, pp. 1310-1318, https://doi.org/10.1177/0146167299258011. [34]

Columbia Center for Teaching and Learning (2020), *Guide for Inclusive Teaching at Columbia,* Columbia University, New York, https://cpb-us-w2.wpmucdn.com/edblogs.columbia.edu/dist/8/1109/files/2020/02/Guide-for-Inclusive-Teaching-at-Columbia_Accessibility-Revisions_15-January-2020_FINAL.pdf (accessed on 2 October 2020). [26]

Council of Ministers of Education, Canada (2020), *Pan-Canadian Global Competencies*. [67]

Curriculum Development Council (2017), *Learning Goals, School Curriculum Framework and Planning, Secondary Education Curriculum Guide*. [66]

Curriculum Development Council (2017), *Secondary Education Curriculum Guide: Booklet 2: Learning Goals, School Curriculum Framework and Planning*. [62]

Dee, T. (2005), "A Teacher like Me: Does Race, Ethnicity, or Gender Matter?", *The American Economic Review,* Vol. 95/2, pp. 158-165, http://www.jstor.org/stable/4132809 (accessed on 12 October 2020). [54]

Dee, T. (2004), "Teachers, race, and student achievement in a randomized experiment", *Review of Economics and Statistics,* Vol. 86/1, pp. 195-210, http://dx.doi.org/10.1162/003465304323023750. [50]

Dewsbury, B. and C. Brame (2019), "Inclusive teaching", *CBE Life Sciences Education*, Vol. 18/2, https://doi.org/10.1187/cbe.19-01-0021. [15]

Egalite, A., B. Kisida and M. Winters (2015), "Representation in the classroom: The effect of own-race teachers on student achievement", *Economics of Education Review,* Vol. 45, pp. 44-52, https://doi.org/10.1016/j.econedurev.2015.01.007. [52]

Florian, L. and K. Black-Hawkins (2011), "Exploring inclusive pedagogy", *British Educational Research Journal,* Vol. 37/5, pp. 813-828, https://doi.org/10.1080/01411926.2010.501096. [11]

Florian, L. and J. Sprat (2013), "Enacting inclusion: a framework for interrogating inclusive practice", *European Journal of Special Needs Education,* Vol. 28/2, pp. 119-135, https://doi.org/10.1080/08856257.2013.778111. [12]

Gay, G. (2010), *Culturally responsive teaching,* Teachers College Press. [33]

Gershenson, S. et al. (2017), "The Long-Run Impacts of Same-Race Teachers", *IZA Discussion Paper,* No. 10630, IZA Institute of Labor Economics, http://ftp.iza.org/dp10630.pdf (accessed on 12 October 2020). [60]

Gershenson, S., S. Holt and N. Papageorge (2016), "Who Believes in Me? The Effect of Student-Teacher Demographic Who Believes in Me? The Effect of Student-Teacher Demographic Match on Teacher Expectations Match on Teacher Expectations", *Economics of Education Review,* Vol. 52, pp. 209-224, https://doi.org/10.17848/wp15-231. [55]

Glaés-Coutts, L. and H. Nilsson (2021), "Who owns the knowledge? Knowledge construction as part of the school improvement process", *Improving Schools 1*, pp. 62-75, https://doi.org/10.1177/1365480220929767. [42]

Goldhaber, D., R. Theobald and C. Tien (2015), "The Theoretical and Empirical Arguments for Diversifying the Teacher Workforce: A Review of the Evidence", *CEDR Policy Brief,* No. 2015-9, Center for Education Data & Research, Seattle, Washington, https://cedr.us/papers/working/CEDR%20WP%202015-9.pdf (accessed on 12 October 2020). [53]

Grissom, J. and C. Redding (2016), "Discretion and Disproportionality", *AERA Open,* Vol. 2/1, pp. 1-25, https://doi.org/10.1177/2332858415622175. [56]

Holt, S. and S. Gershenson (2019), "The Impact of Demographic Representation on Absences and Suspensions", *Policy Studies Journal,* Vol. 47/4, pp. 1069-1099, https://doi.org/10.1111/psj.12229. [58]

Kenyon, A. (2018), *Best Practices for Inclusive Assessment,* Duke University Learning Innovation, https://learninginnovation.duke.edu/blog/2018/11/inclusive-assessment/ (accessed on 2 October 2020). [25]

Lindsay, C. and C. Hart (2017), "Exposure to Same-Race Teachers and Student Disciplinary Outcomes for Black Students in North Carolina", *Educational Evaluation and Policy Analysis*, Vol. 39/3, pp. 485-510, https://doi.org/10.3102/0162373717693109. [59]

McLeskey, J., B. Billingsley and N. Waldron (2016), *Principal Leadership for Effective Inclusive Schools*, Emerald Group Publishing Limited, https://doi.org/10.1108/S0270-401320160000032005. [38]

New Brunswick Department of Education and Early Childhood Development (2013), *Policy 322*, https://www2.gnb.ca/content/dam/gnb/Departments/ed/pdf/K12/policies-politiques/e/322A.pdf. [40]

New Zealand Ministry of Education (2013), *Effective governance: Building inclusive schools,* https://www.nzsta.org.nz/assets/Governance/Effective-governance-publications-and-resources/Building-inclusive-schools.pdf. [43]

OECD (2019), *Making Physical Education Dynamic and Inclusive for 2030: International Curriculum Analysis,* OECD Publishing, Paris, https://www.oecd.org/education/2030-project/contact/OECD_FUTURE_OF_EDUCATION_2030_MAKING_PHYSICAL_DYNAMIC_AND_INCLUSIVE_FOR_2030.pdf (accessed on 2 October 2020). [22]

OECD (2019), "Supporting and guiding novice teachers: Evidence from TALIS 2018", *Teaching in Focus*, No. 29, OECD Publishing, Paris, https://dx.doi.org/10.1787/fe6c9c0c-en. [44]

OECD (2019), *TALIS 2018 Results (Volume I): Teachers and School Leaders as Lifelong Learners*, TALIS, OECD Publishing, Paris, https://dx.doi.org/10.1787/1d0bc92a-en. [47]

OECD (2018), *Effective Teacher Policies: Insights from PISA*, PISA, OECD Publishing, Paris, https://dx.doi.org/10.1787/9789264301603-en. [45]

OECD (2018), *PISA 2018 Results*, OECD Publishing, Paris, https://doi.org/10.1787/d5f68679-en. [63]

OECD (2018), *The Resilience of Students with an Immigrant Background: Factors that Shape Well-being*, OECD Reviews of Migrant Education, OECD Publishing, Paris, https://dx.doi.org/10.1787/9789264292093-en. [36]

OECD (2017), *Teachers in Diverse Societies: Proceedings of the Second Policy Forum*, OECD Publishing, Paris, http://www.oecd.org/education/school/Forum-Proceedings-final.pdf. [46]

OECD (2015), *PISA 2015 Results: Students' Well-Being*, OECD Publishing, Paris, https://doi.org/10.1787/9789264273856-en. [64]

OECD (2008), "Assessment for Learning Formative Assessment", *OECD/CERI International Conference "Learning in the 21st Century: Research, Innovation and Policy"*, OECD Publishing, Paris, https://www.oecd.org/site/educeri21st/40600533.pdf (accessed on 2 October 2020). [24]

O'neill, D., D. McDonald and S. Jones (2018), "Toying with inclusivity", *BMJ*, Vol. 363, https://doi.org/10.1136/bmj.k519. [18]

Ouazad, A. (2014), "Assessed by a teacher like me: Race and teacher assessments", *Education Finance and Policy*, Vol. 9/3, pp. 334-372, https://doi.org/10.1162/EDFP_a_00136. [57]

Perlman, M., T. Kankesan and J. Zhang (2010), "Promoting diversity in early child care education", *Early Child Development and Care*, Vol. 180/6, pp. 753-766, https://doi.org/10.1080/03004430802287606. [19]

Peterson, A. et al. (2018), "Understanding innovative pedagogies: Key themes to analyse new approaches to teaching and learning", *OECD Education Working Papers*, No. 172, OECD Publishing, Paris, https://dx.doi.org/10.1787/9f843a6e-en. [10]

Postareff, L., S. Lindblom-Ylänne and A. Nevgi (2007), "The effect of pedagogical training on teaching in higher education", *Teaching and Teacher Education*, Vol. 23/5, pp. 557-571, https://doi.org/10.1016/j.tate.2006.11.013. [29]

Riehl, C. (2000), "The Principal's Role in Creating Inclusive Schools for Diverse Students: A Review of Normative, Empirical, and Critical Literature on the Practice of Educational Administration", *Review of Educational Research*, Vol. 70/1, pp. 55-81, https://doi.org/10.3102%2F00346543070001055. [39]

Rodriguez, J. et al. (2020), "On the Shoulders of Giants: Benefits of Participating in a Dialogic Professional Development Program for In-Service Teachers", *Front. Psychol.*, Vol. 11/5, https://doi.org/10.3389/fpsyg.2020.00005. [31]

Sanger, C. and N. Gleason (eds.) (2020), *Inclusive Pedagogy and Universal Design Approaches for Diverse Learning Environments*, Palgrave Macmillan, https://doi.org/10.1007/978-981-15-1628-3_2. [14]

Schleicher, A. (2020), *Insights and Interpretations TALIS 2018 Teaching and Learning International Survey*, OECD, Paris, http://www.oecd.org/education/talis/TALIS2018_insights_and_interpretations.pdf (accessed on 24 September 2020). [48]

Science, D. (2017), *Students' Profile by the End of Compulsory Schooling*. [65]

Seah, K. (2018), "Immigrant educators and students' academic achievement", *Labour Economics*, Vol. 51/C, pp. 152-169, https://doi.org/10.1016/j.labeco.2017.12.007. [61]

Straske, M. (2019), *If You Give a Boy a Baby: Encouraging Empathy in Preschool Boys through Toy Play and Emotion Talk,* Washington and Lee University, Washington, https://dspace.wlu.edu/handle/11021/34433 (accessed on 2 October 2020). [20]

UNESCO (2020), *Inclusive Curriculum*, International Bureau of Education, http://www.ibe.unesco.org/en/glossary-curriculum-terminology/i/inclusive-curriculum (accessed on 2 October 2020). [17]

UNESCO (2020), *Inclusive Teaching: Preparing all teachers to teach all students,* UNESCO, https://unesdoc.unesco.org/ark:/48223/pf0000374447. [41]

Wong, W. and M. Hines (2015), "Effects of Gender Color-Coding on Toddlers' Gender-Typical Toy Play", *Archives of Sexual Behavior,* Vol. 44/5, pp. 1233-1242, https://doi.org/10.1007/s10508-014-0400-5. [21]

Yale, P. (n.d.), *Classroom Seating Arrangements*, https://poorvucenter.yale.edu/ClassroomSeatingArrangements. [37]

Yeager, D., G. Walton and G. Cohen (2013), "Addressing Achievement Gaps with Psychological Interventions", *Phi Delta Kappan*, Vol. 94/5, pp. 62-65, https://doi.org/10.1177/003172171309400514. [35]

Youcubed - Stanford Graduate School of Education (2020), *Youcubed*, https://www.youcubed.org/mathematical-mindset-teaching-resources/ (accessed on 26 October 2020). [16]

Zirkel, S. (2008), "The influence of multicultural educational practices on student outcomes and intergroup relations", *The Teachers College Record,* Vol. 110, pp. 1147-1181. [32]

www.ingramcontent.com/pod-product-compliance
Lightning Source LLC
LaVergne TN
LVHW061949070526
838199LV00060B/4039